THE GREAT BIG BOOK OF COMPUTING

Copyright © QED Publishing 2009

First published in the UK in 2009 by
QED Publishing
A Quarto Group company
226 City Road
London EC1V 2TT

www.qed-publishing.co.uk

All rights reserved. No part of this publication may be reproduced, stored in a retrieval system, or transmitted in any form or by any means, electronic, mechanical, photocopying, recording, or otherwise, without the prior permission of the publisher, nor be otherwise circulated in any form of binding or cover other than that in which it is published and without a similar condition being imposed on the subsequent purchaser.

A catalogue record for this book is available from the British Library.

ISBN 978 1 84835 285 8

Printed and bound in China

Author Anne Rooney
Consultant Philip Stubbs
Editor Anna Claybourne
Designer Jacqueline Palmer
Photographer Ray Moller
Illustrator John Haslam

Publisher Steve Evans
Creative Director Zeta Davies
Managing Editor Amanda Askew

Words in **bold** can be found in the glossary on page 152.

THE GREAT BIG BOOK OF COMPUTING

ANNE ROONEY

QED Publishing

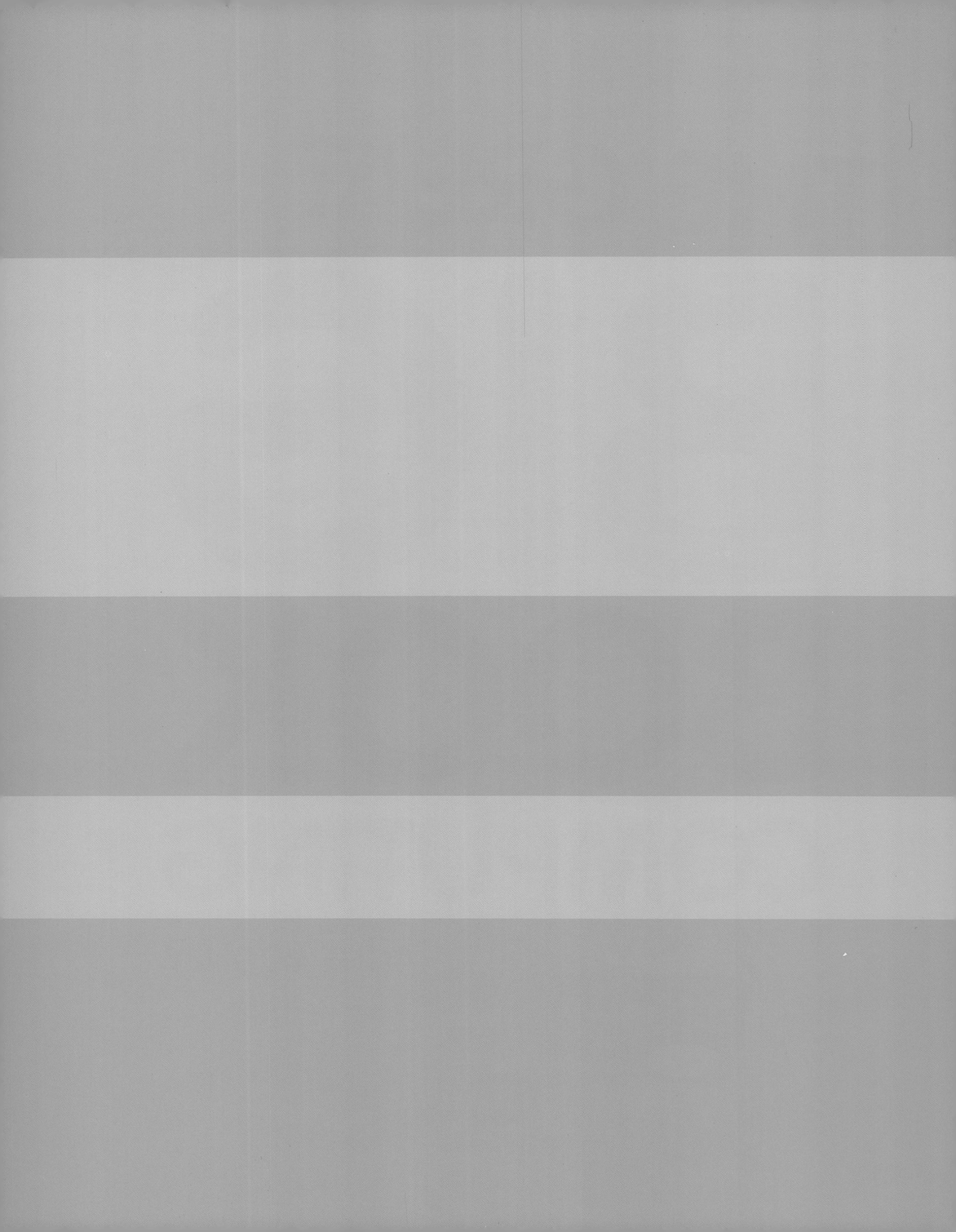

CONTENTS

FINDING AND SORTING INFORMATION

What's it all about?	**10**
How does it work?	**12**
Paper or computer?	**14**
Build your own database	**16**
Starting your database	**18**
Making it work	**20**
Looking up facts	**22**
The world's biggest database	**24**
Finding what you want	**26**
Checking your facts	**28**
Sharing information	**30**

COMMUNITCATING ONLINE

What's it all about?	**34**
Sending messages	**36**
Think ahead	**38**
One-to-one	**40**
You've got mail!	**42**
The address book	**44**
Attachments	**46**
Share the message	**48**
Looking good	**50**
Make a sound	**52**
Adding sound and pictures	**54**

WRITING PROGRAMS

What's it all about?	**58**
How does it work?	**60**
What do you want to do?	**62**
Writing instructions	**64**
Do it again!	**66**
Make a pattern	**68**
Testing, testing	**70**
Planning a sequence	**72**
Triggering events	**74**
On and on and on...	**76**
Perfect!	**78**

PICTURES, PHOTOS AND PAINTINGS

What's it all about?	**82**
Think first	**84**
Paintings	**86**
All change!	**88**
Working with photos	**90**
Drawings	**92**
Making changes	**94**
Pile it up	**96**
Making plans	**98**
Make a model	**100**
Perfect!	**102**

SPREADSHEETS, GRAPHS AND CHARTS

What's it all about?	**106**
How does it work?	**108**
Make your own spreadsheet	**110**
Working with data	**112**
Sorting it out	**114**
Graphs and charts	**116**
Filtered facts	**118**
Simulations	**120**
All change!	**122**
Finding patterns	**124**
Perfect!	**126**

INVITES, POSTERS AND PRESENTATIONS

What's it all about?	**130**
How does it work?	**132**
Getting started	**134**
Making sense	**136**
Organizing information	**138**
Looking good	**140**
Text effects, styles and sizes	**141**
Pictures	**142**
Arranging text	**146**
Page layout	**148**
Perfect!	**150**

Glossary	**152**
Index	**156**

FINDING AND SORTING INFORMATION

What's it all about?

Do you know what goes on in your brain? It's a huge information factory. During your life you'll use it to learn lots of facts, make connections between them and store the ones you need to remember.

Brains and computers

You can store a huge amount of information in your brain – and there's loads you can do with it.

However, no one can remember everything they've ever learned, and we soon forget information we don't use very often. That's where a computer can help.

Full of facts

A computer system for storing, comparing and sorting facts is called a database. A database can be very small, and keep a specific set of facts – such as the heights of all the children in a class. Or it can be very large and store huge amounts of information – such as details of every movie ever made.

Ready to go?

In this book you'll find out how to use databases to store, find and work with information in lots of different ways. You'll make databases of your own to work with information you've gathered, and you'll use the World Wide Web to collect even more facts.

How does it work?

Usually, a database groups together information that's related in some way. For example, it could store information about the members of a club or the things for sale in a shop.

Everyday databases

You could make a database of all your CDs, listing all the artists, all the songs and when each CD was released. Your school has a database of information about all the pupils. It has details like your name, address and date of birth. If you belong to a fan club or library, or subscribe to a magazine, it probably has a database of all its members, too.

There are databases all around us in our everyday lives. If you use an encyclopedia on CD-ROM, that's a database. And if you buy things in a shop and use a loyalty card, the shop's database keeps a record of what you've bought.

12

Fact-finding

Storing lots of information is all very well, but unless you can find the facts you want easily, it's not much use.

Imagine a big book of facts without an index. You know there's lots of information in there, but how are you going to find out what you need to know? Without an index, you'd just have to read through each page in turn. It would take a very long time. Encyclopedias and phone books are arranged in alphabetical order.

Databases, too, need ways to help you to find information. Unlike a book, a database can change the order it shows you information. For example, you could look at a list of kings and queens in alphabetical or chronological order.

Paper or computer?

In all your work, it's worth thinking about whether you really need to use the computer, or whether there might be a better way. For working with facts and figures, a database on the computer is often best.

Basketball scores
Ty 'Springer' Daniels 24 goals
Zeb Watson 29 goals
'Tall Paul' McCoy 3 goals
AJ Elliot

Sporting heroes

Imagine you want to keep a list of the top players in a particular sport, and how many goals each has scored. As more matches are played, you add more details.

If you kept your notes on paper, you'd have to decide how to list the players – by team or alphabetically by name. You'd also need to add up the scores for each player. This would change each week, so you'd have to work them out all over again.

If you kept your list on the computer, it could add up all the goals for you, and tell you who had the best score so far every week.

This week's results...

You could use your sports data to make a set of collector's cards – one on each player.

How computers help

Keeping a database on a computer helps in several different ways:

The computer can automatically compare facts or do calculations for you. On paper, you'd have to look through them all and do the sums yourself.

You can easily sort information into any order, almost instantly. If you keep a list on paper, it takes some time to re-order your facts.

You can print out your information any time you add new facts. On paper, you'd have to copy it all out again each time.

A computer can find information very quickly, but on paper you have to read through the whole lot to find what you want.

Sometimes, though, a paper list may be better. You can carry it around easily with you, use it when you can't get to the computer, and add your own pictures or stickers.

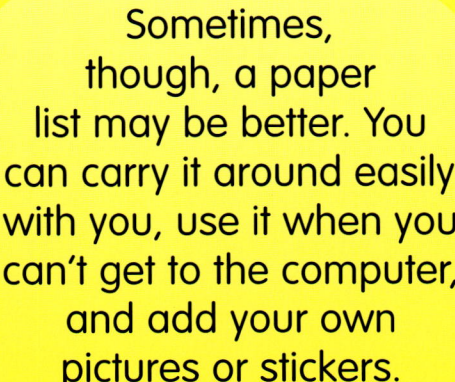

Build your own database

If you have a database program on your computer, you can start making your own databases. You might make a database to help with a hobby or as part of your schoolwork.

Think first

Before you start making your database, work out what information you want to put in it. You might have the information handy, or you might have to collect facts for your database.

Doing a survey

One way to get information is to do a survey. You can draw up a list of questions on paper. If there are only a few possible answers to a question, use multiple choice questions with tick boxes for different options.

Survey questions

Make sure you ask relevant questions. For example, if you're finding out about cool places, it's not relevant to ask people what their favourite colour is.

Make your questions as useful as possible. Ask for date of birth, not age. Ages change every year, but a database can work out ages from dates of birth.

Date of birth 25 May 1999 – age 10

Date of birth 19 July 1987 – age 22

Date of birth 31 April 1947 – age 62

16

Question time

Imagine you wanted to make a database of fun things to do in your town. You'd work out the best questions, then make them into a data collection sheet.

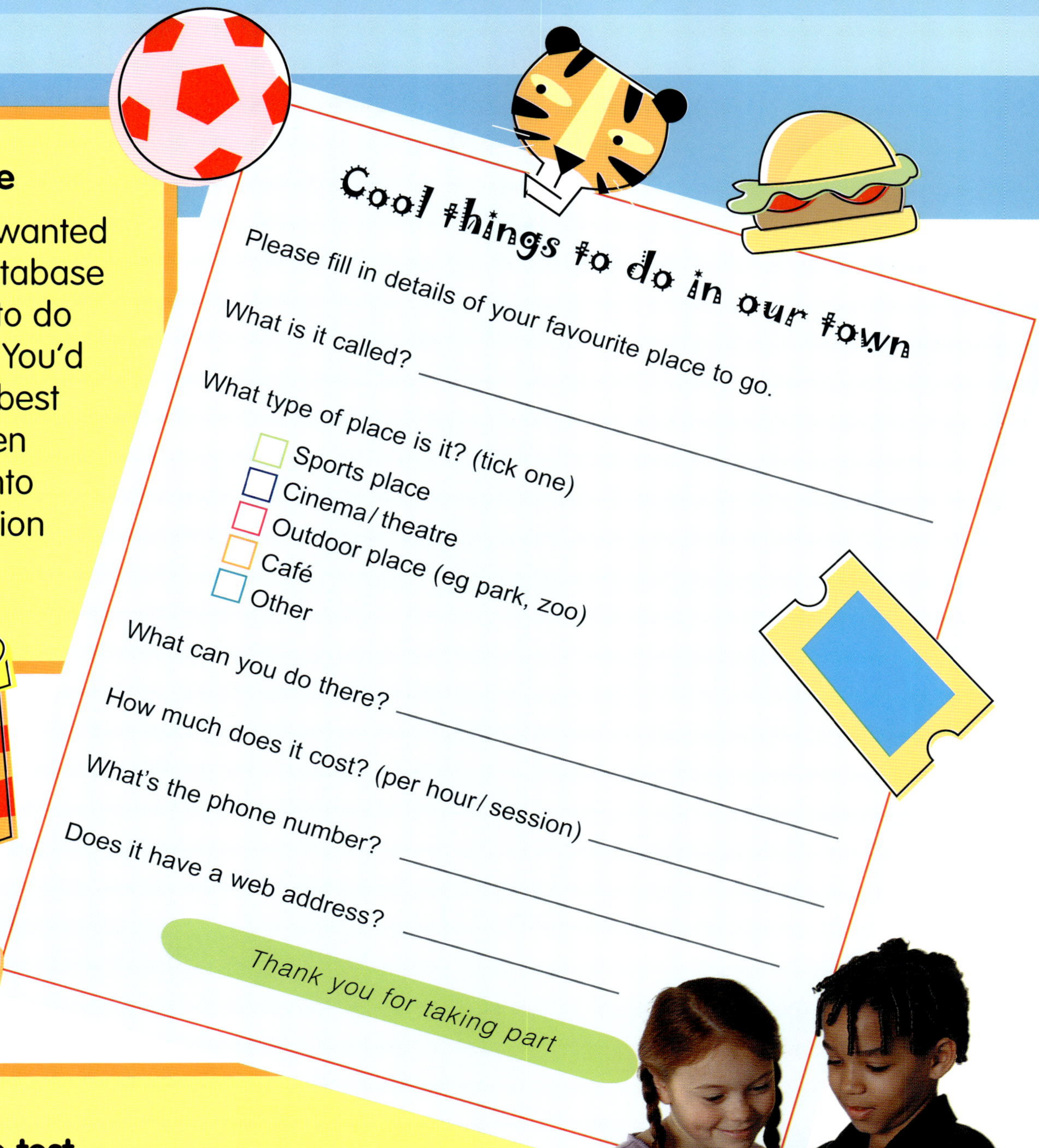

Cool things to do in our town

Please fill in details of your favourite place to go.

What is it called? _____

What type of place is it? (tick one)
- ☐ Sports place
- ☐ Cinema/theatre
- ☐ Outdoor place (eg park, zoo)
- ☐ Café
- ☐ Other

What can you do there? _____

How much does it cost? (per hour/session) _____

What's the phone number? _____

Does it have a web address? _____

Thank you for taking part

Put it to the test

Next, decide who to include in your survey. Is your database only for young people, or should you ask people of all ages? Then, think about all the answers you might get and see if any of your questions could be better. For example, people might just answer 'yes' to the last question – so you might change it to 'What is the web address?'.

Starting your database

Once you've collected all the information you need, you can make a start on building your database.

Records and fields

A database divides information up into records and fields.

Each thing for which you have information has its own record. In a database of cars, there'd be one record for each car.

Each fact in a record goes in a space called a field. In your car database, each record might have fields for the make, model and engine size of the car.

If you made a database of horses at a stable, you'd have a record for each horse, with fields for, say, the name, the date of birth (D.O.B), the eight and the colour of the horse.

DO IT!

Using your database software, start a new database. The first thing to do is set up the types of fields that will be used in each record and give each field a name, such as 'Date of birth' or 'Phone number'.

You'll need to choose the type of field – for instance, numbers, text or dates.

Name: Tora
D.o.B: 21.12.99
Height: 15 hands
Colour: brown

18

Putting in your information

You put information into your database by typing in the fields on each record.

You'll need to make a new record for each item you have information about.

Check the information is correct before you enter it, and copy it into the computer carefully. The computer can't correct mistakes for you and you'll get the wrong answers out of the database if you put the wrong information in. When you've finished, print everything out and check it.

Cool places

- Record → Venue name
- Field → Greenhill Sports Centre
- Name of field → Venue type
- Tick box →
  - ☒ Sports place
  - ☐ Cinema/theatre
  - ☐ Outdoor place (eg park, zoo)
  - ☐ Café
  - ☐ Other
- Information as text → Facilities: swimming pool, gymnasium, football pitch, baseball pitch
- Information as numbers → Cost per hour/session: £ 5.50
- Phone number: 01111 22222
- Web address: www.greenhillsports.com

19

Making it work

Once you've put all your information into your database you can make lists, graphs or charts from it.

Putting things in order

You can look at the information in your database in different ways by asking the database to put the records in order for you. This is called sorting the database.

For example, you might want your 'Cool places' database to show you a list of places in order of price, with the cheapest first. To do this, you'd need to:

• Choose the field you want to see information about – in this case, it's the 'Cost' field.

• Tell the computer how to sort the information. To see the cheapest prices first, tell the computer to list the entries in order of cost.

DO IT!

In your database program, the option to sort your database will probably be called 'Sort' or 'Reorder'. You should be able to choose ascending order (going up, for example from A–Z or from 1–9) or descending order (going down, from Z–A or from 9–1).

You can print out a list of the information in the order you've chosen.

Screen Ultramarine £2.50
Finn's Funfair £3.25
Movieland £3.70
Jedley Zoo £5
Greenhill Sports £5.50

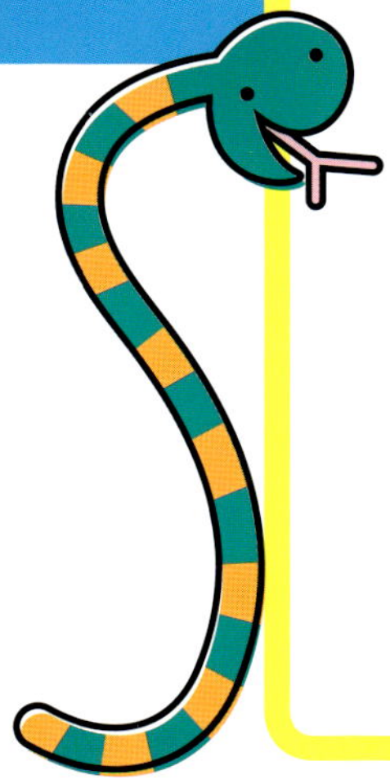

Graphs and charts

Most databases will let you make a graph, using the information stored in them. It's often easier to see facts by looking at a graph than by reading numbers.

Imagine you had a database on people's pets. You could get the database to draw a graph to show how many children in your class had each type of pet.

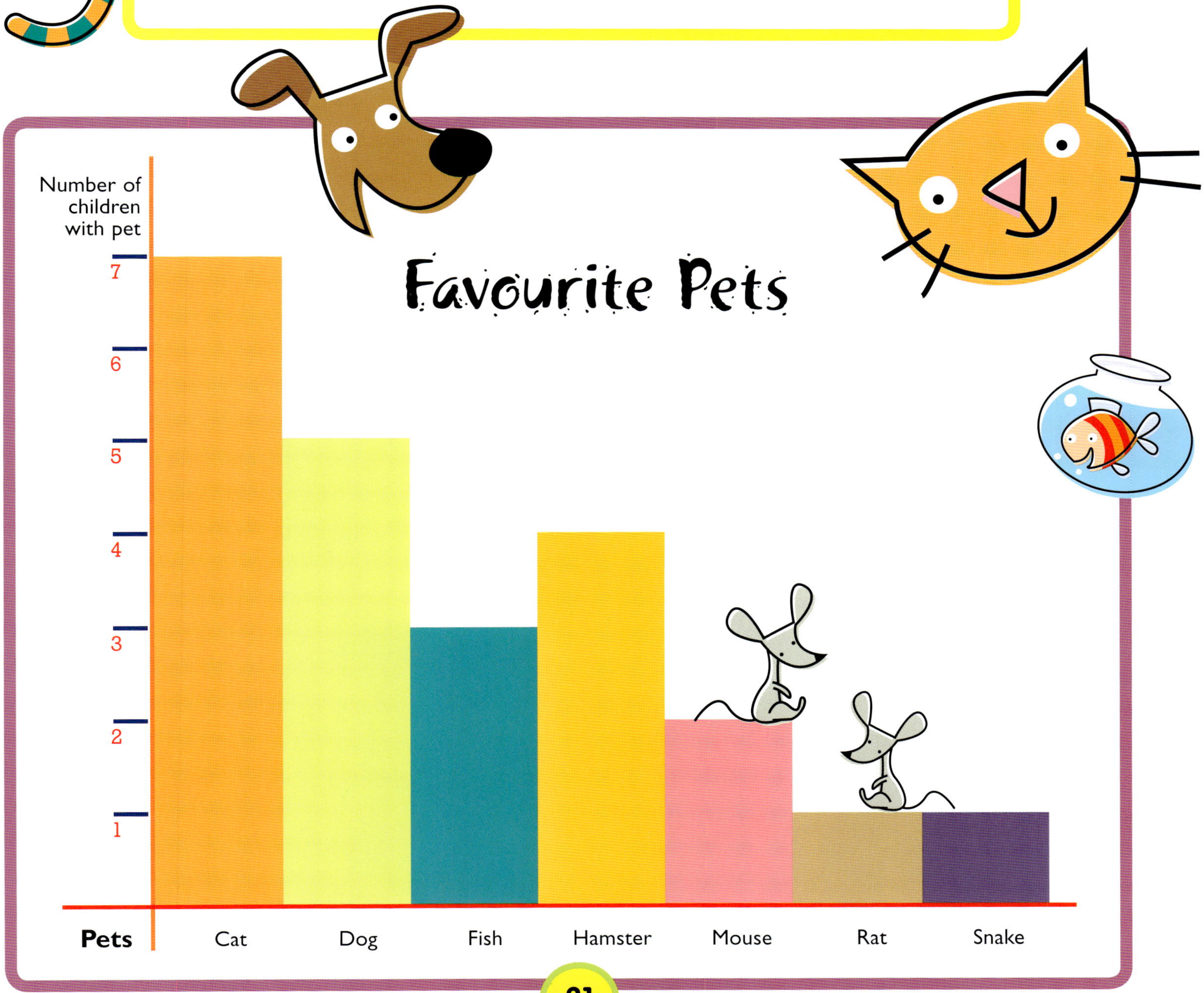

Favourite Pets

Number of children with pet

| Pets | Cat | Dog | Fish | Hamster | Mouse | Rat | Snake |

Looking up facts

Sometimes you will want to find particular items in a database. You'll need to tell the database what you're looking for and ask it to find anything that matches.

Ask the database

Suppose you want to use your 'Cool places' database to find all the sports places, or all the cinemas. You find them by asking the database a question called a *query*, or by setting a *filter*.

To do this, you usually have to fill in a form on screen showing what you want to find. The computer will look for things in the fields you fill in. It will ignore any fields you leave blank.

For example, you could look for cinemas like this:

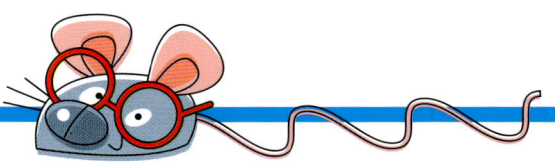

Venue name

Venue type
☐ Sports place
☒ Cinema/theatre
☐ Outdoor place (eg park, zoo)
☐ Cafe
☐ Other

Facilities

Cost per hour/session
£

Phone number

Web address

22

Finding out more

What if you want to find something more specific – such as all cinemas that cost less than £5?

For things like this, you can use special symbols, called operators, to find numbers in a particular range.

This search would find cinemas that cost less than £5.

Operators include:

= means equals
eg Cost = £5
means 'find prices that are exactly £5'

> means more than
eg Cost > £5
means 'find prices over £5'

< means less than
eg Cost < £5
means 'find prices under £5'

Make it match

In some databases, you search for results by entering a whole phrase, such as Cost <£5, into a search box. Make sure you always use the same words the database uses. For example, if a field is named Cost, you must use the word Cost, not a different word like price, because the computer won't recognize it.

Does not compute...!

23

The world's biggest database

The biggest database in the world is the World Wide Web. Everything you want to know is probably out there somewhere!

Get started on the Web

To use the World Wide Web, you need to make sure your computer is connected to the Internet, and start up a web browser, such as Internet Explorer or Netscape. Ask for help if you're not sure how to do this.

Starting from home

The page your web browser shows when it starts up is called your home page. You can always get back to it by clicking the Home button in your browser.

Moving around

If you know which web page you want to look at, type in its web address accurately, and then press the Enter or Return key.

Web links

When you get to the page you want, there might be links to other useful information. A link is usually underlined and shown in a different colour, like this: Great white shark.

Going back

If you end up somewhere you don't want to be, or see something you're not comfortable with, click on the Back button to go back a page, or on the Home button to start again.

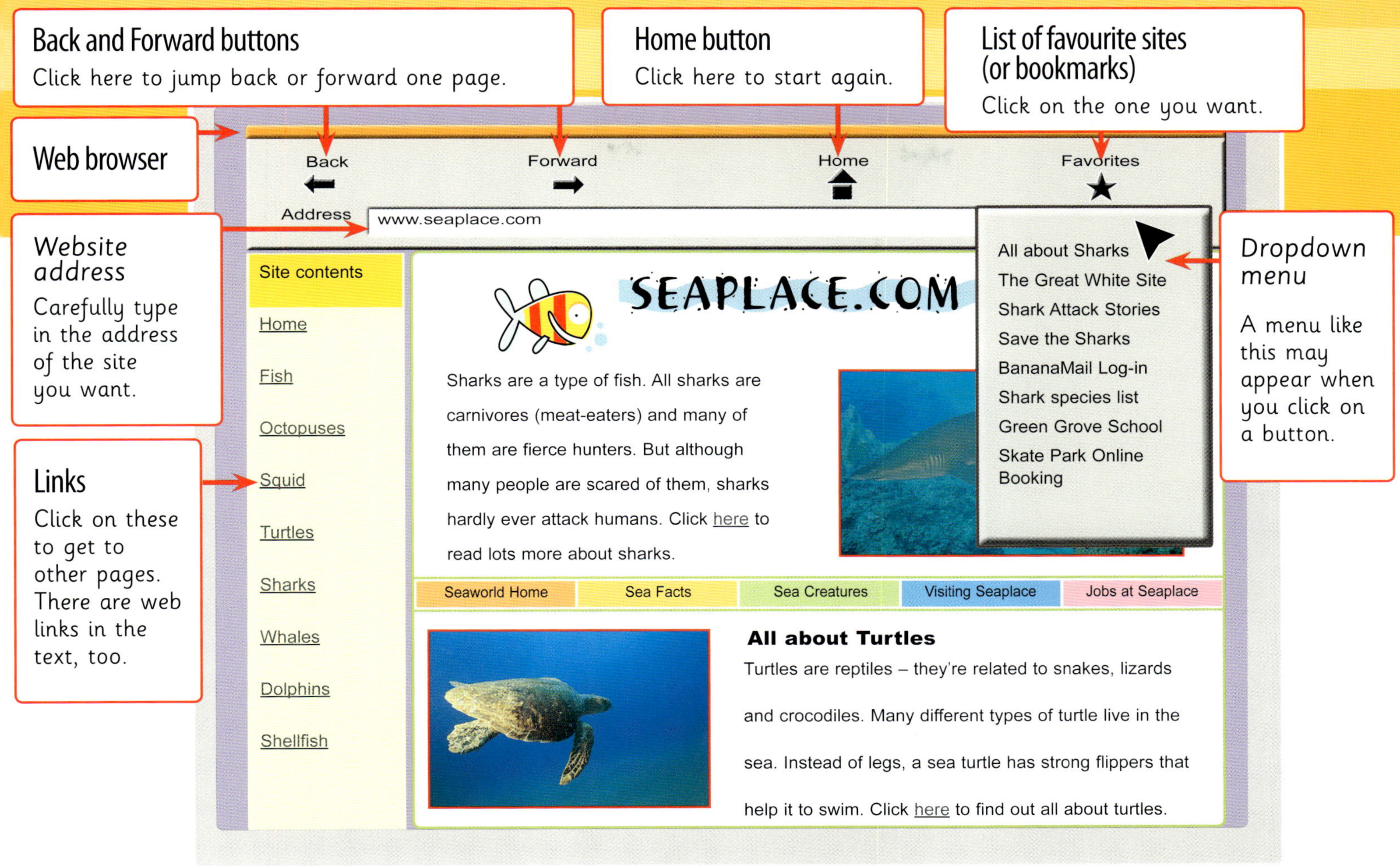

Back and Forward buttons
Click here to jump back or forward one page.

Home button
Click here to start again.

List of favourite sites (or bookmarks)
Click on the one you want.

Web browser

Website address
Carefully type in the address of the site you want.

Dropdown menu
A menu like this may appear when you click on a button.

Links
Click on these to get to other pages. There are web links in the text, too.

Best places

If you find a web page you like, and you think you might want to use it again, you can add it to a list of your favourite sites. If you're using Internet Explorer, these are called Favorites, and if you're using Netscape they're called Bookmarks.

'Favorites' is spelled the American way because Internet Explorer is made by an American company!

DO IT!

Open the Bookmarks or Favorites menu in your browser, and click on 'Add' to add the page to your list. Remember what the page is called in the list, so that you can find it again later.

When you want to go back to it again, open the menu. Then click on the name of the page you want to go back to.

25

Finding what you want

There are two ways of finding what you want on the Web. You can do a search, or you can use a contents list or directory, which lets you choose from different categories of information.

Working with directories

A directory page lists categories of information, such as 'news', 'sport', 'schoolwork help' and 'entertainment'. When you click on one, a list for that topic appears for you to choose again. Eventually, you should get to what you want.

A directory is good if you know roughly what you want to find. If you want to read the latest news, or see which movies are just coming out, a directory can help.

DO IT!

Try these directory pages:
www.yahooligans.com
www.kidgrid.com
http://directory.google.com
(click on 'Kids and Teens')

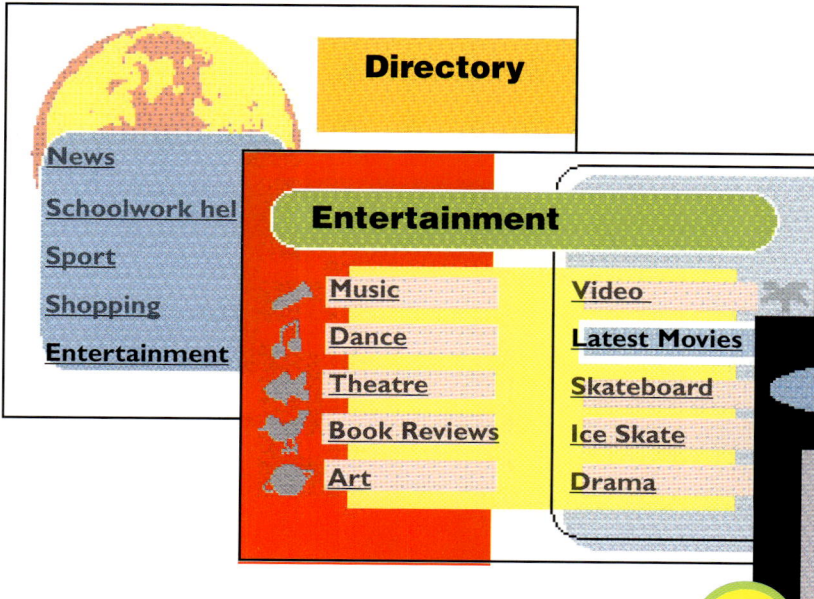

26

Searching the Web

To find precise information, say a cake recipe, a search is better.

You search the Web using a special kind of web page called a search page or *search engine*.

You'll need to type in the words you're looking for (called *keywords*), and click a button to start the search. The search engine will list pages that contain your keywords.

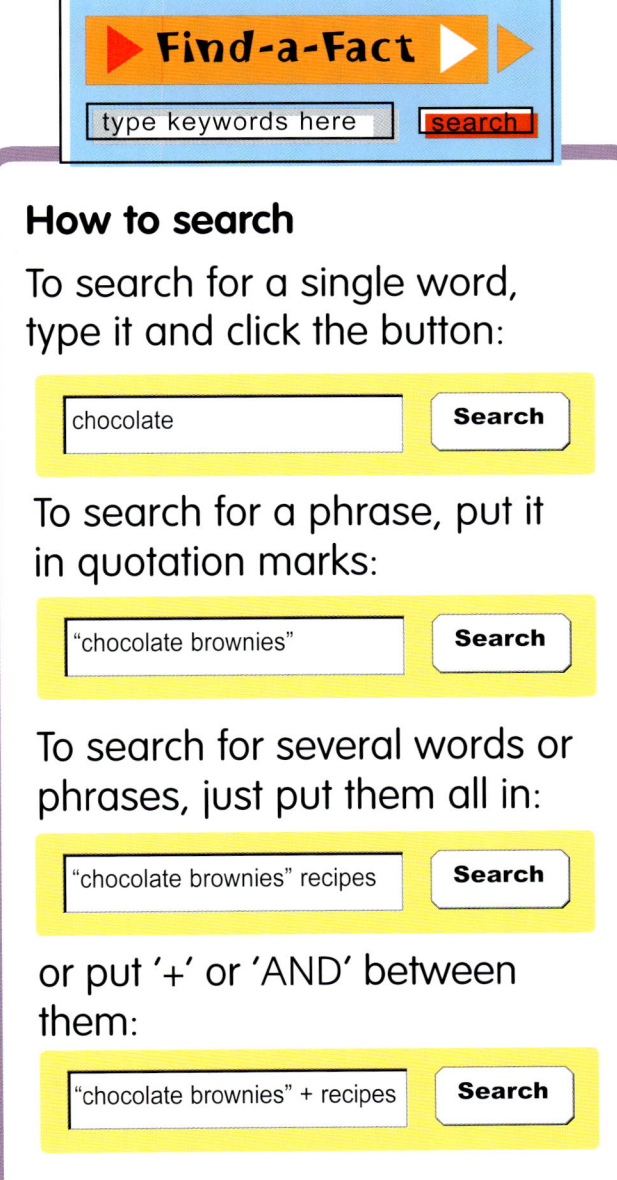

How to search

To search for a single word, type it and click the button:

| chocolate | **Search** |

To search for a phrase, put it in quotation marks:

| "chocolate brownies" | **Search** |

To search for several words or phrases, just put them all in:

| "chocolate brownies" recipes | **Search** |

or put '+' or 'AND' between them:

| "chocolate brownies" + recipes | **Search** |

DO IT!
Try these search pages:
www.google.com
www.yahoo.com
www.alltheweb.com
www.altavista.com

Choosing the best keywords takes practice. Don't search for "how to make chocolate brownies" because unless a web page has that exact phrase in it, you won't find anything. But don't be too vague, either. If you just put "recipes" you'd find thousands of pages and it would take you ages to track down brownies!

Checking your facts

 Whether you've found information from your own database, from a CD-ROM or from the Web, you need to have a good look at it and decide whether it's what you need.

Asking questions

Whatever you're going to do with the information you've found, you'll need to check that it's:

• Accurate • Reliable • Relevant

Make sure you think about all these things before you use the information you've found.

Accuracy

You can probably trust information you get from an encyclopedia or a CD-ROM to be accurate.

If it's from your own database, it will be right as long as you put in the right information and asked the right questions – so check! Think about the answers you'd expect to get, and if they're very different, check your work again.

• Reliable – do you trust the place you got it from?

• Accurate – is it right?

• Relevant – is it suitable for what you want to use it for?

Reliability

If the information is from the Web, is it from a website you can trust? Anyone can put up web pages and no one checks that they're accurate or true.

The information on websites can be biased too. This means that the people who put up the website want you to think in a particular way.

Relevance

You might find some very interesting information, but if it isn't anything to do with the topic you're working on it's not relevant – so leave it out!

I can trust this Encarta CD-ROM.

This protest site 'Fight Pollution' may be biased... But 'The SciTech Museum Kid's Page - Pollution' looks good!

That's a cool pic of Dolly the cloned sheep! But I can't really put that in because it's not about pollution...

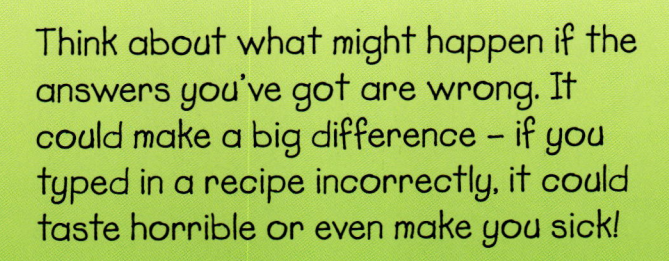

Think about what might happen if the answers you've got are wrong. It could make a big difference – if you typed in a recipe incorrectly, it could taste horrible or even make you sick!

Sharing information

Storing lots of information is only the start. You need to do things with it – like presenting it in a way other people can understand, or printing it out to use later.

Database reports

If you're working with a database of your own, you can print out *reports* which show some or all of the information it stores.

Before printing out your report, you may be able to choose different text styles and arrangements to make it look smarter.

Chocolate recipes

Recipe	Time it takes to make
Chocolate sauce	5 mins
Choc crispies	10 mins
Choco-cherry cookies	15 mins
Choc'n'flake cake	1 hour
Chocolate ice-cream	6 hours

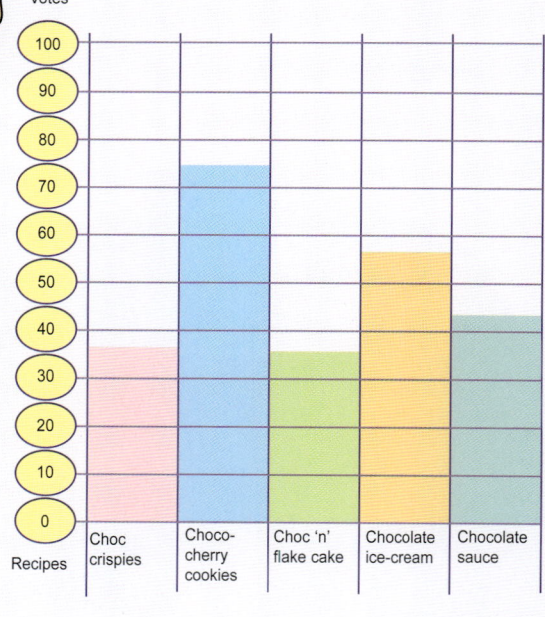

TOP TEN chocolate recipes survey

Information from the Web

If you're working with information from the Web – or from another large database such as a CD-ROM – you'll need to copy, save or print the information you've found so you can use it for your projects.

You can:

• Print a page out, so you can show it to other people or look at it later.

• Save the page on your computer so that you can look at it without having to connect to the Internet or load the CD.

• Copy words and pictures from a page to put into your own work.

Don't steal!

Words and pictures on the Web are someone else's work, and the law protects other people's work. It's OK to use a bit in something that's just for you, but you can't make lots of copies or include it in a book or a website without getting permission.

DO IT!

To copy information from the Web, use the mouse to select the words or pictures you want. Choose 'Copy' from the menus at the top of the browser window. Then open a document of your own, and use the 'Paste' option to stick in the bits you've copied.

When you copy something from the Web to use in your own projects, always add a note of the web address where you found it. This will make it easy to check it again later, and will show you're not pretending it's your own work.

COMMUNICATING ONLINE

What's it all about?

Do you use the computer to communicate with other people? You might send email, use a kids' chat or messaging service, look at web pages – or maybe make your own web pages or multimedia projects.

This time it's personal

When you send an email message, it's usually to someone you know, or at least someone whose name you know. It's a personal communication – something just between you and the other person. You can send the same email message to several people – to invite them to a party, for example – but it's still just between you and a few other people who you know.

Free-for-all

When you look at a web page, or even make your own, you're involved in a different kind of communication. You usually don't know the person who's made the web pages you look at. If you make your own web pages, you don't know the people who will look at them. Communications intended for lots of people are called *mass communications*.

In this book you'll find out about communicating with people you know, using email, and communicating with lots of people using web pages and multimedia.

Sending messages

Communicating with people using the computer is quite new. Before the 1990s, most people kept in touch by letter or phone. Mass communications were by radio, television, books and newspapers.

Early messages

Hundreds of years ago, there were no telephones, radios or televisions. To communicate over long distances, people had to use letters, or send messages using things like flags, smoke signals or drums.

In private

You couldn't have a very private conversation by smoke signal – lots of people could see it! Private communications in the past had to be sent by sealed letter. Sometimes they were even written in code, so that if anyone looked at the letter they couldn't see immediately what it said.

A message to keep

If you have a letter, you can keep it and look at it later. You can't do that with a phone call or a message sent by drums or flags. In the same way, you can keep an email, and you can print it if you want a copy to show other people or to put away.

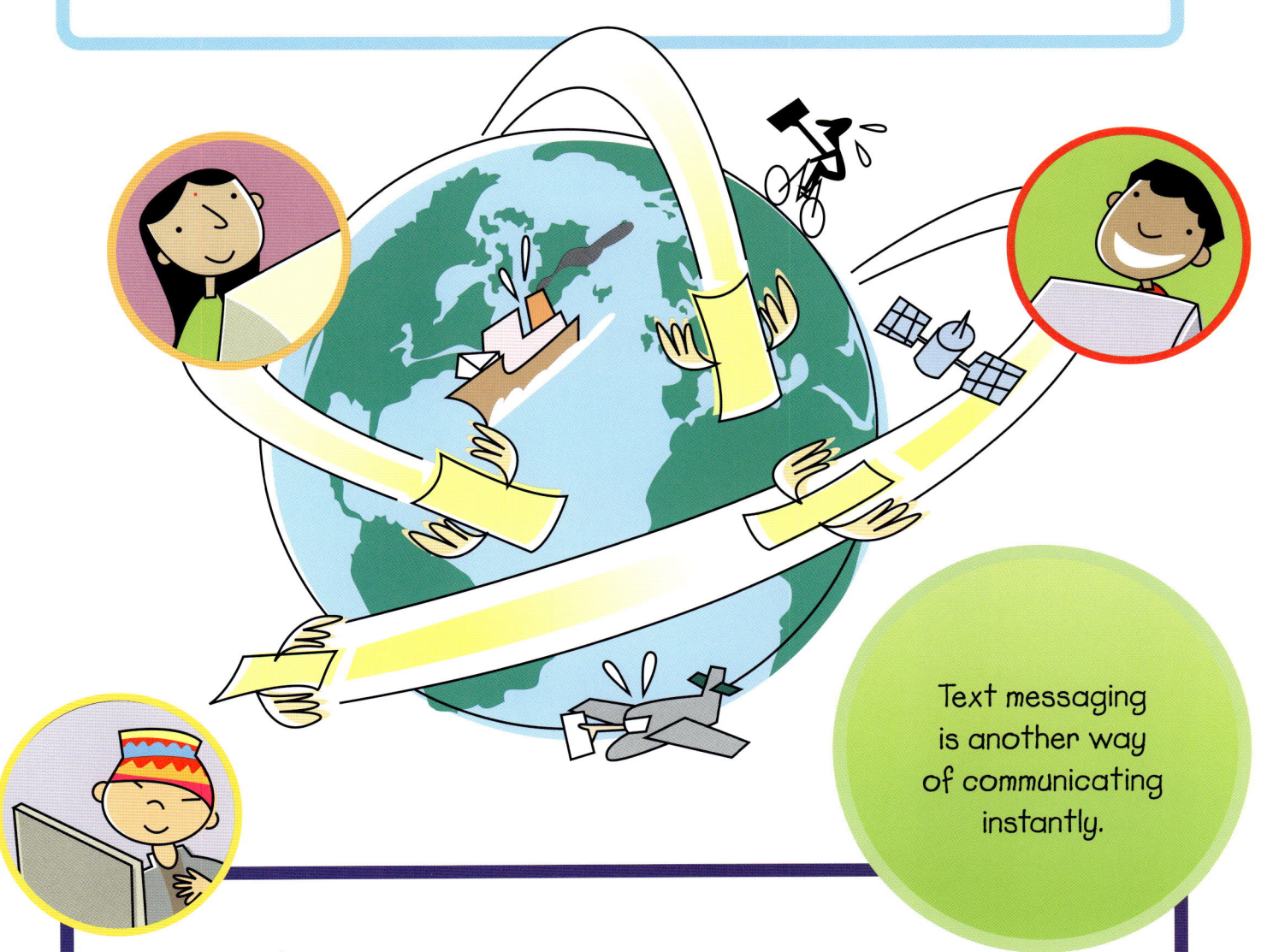

Text messaging is another way of communicating instantly.

Top speed

Email is a very quick way of keeping in touch. Seconds after the message leaves your computer, it arrives at its destination, even if that's on the other side of the world. But to get a letter from Europe to China takes several days if it goes by plane, or weeks by sea.

Think ahead

Before you start any message, you should think about what you want to say and who you want to say it to. And think about whether using the computer is the best way – sometimes it might be better to phone or write a letter.

Multimedia

You've probably used CD-ROMs or websites that have a mixture of words, pictures, sounds and maybe even bits of movie. This is called multimedia. It's a great way of getting a message across, as you can use lots of different methods. If you wrote an essay on paper about, say, farm animals, you could use words and draw pictures. But on the computer you could make a multimedia page with the sounds the animals make and maybe even a video of them, too.

All about pigs

Click to:
- See pig photos
- Hear pig sounds
- Watch the pig video!

The pigs kept on farms today are descended from wild boars.

Tell the world

If you make a multimedia show and put it on a web page, people all around the world can see it. The Web is the only way that you can quickly let anyone in the world see your work.

TAKE CARE

The Internet is used by lots of people, and some use it for things that aren't very nice. Make sure that a grown-up is with you while you are using the Web. Always check with a grown-up before reading email from someone you don't know, and never give your full name or address in an email message or on a web page. If you see something that upsets you, tell your teacher or parent.

One-to-one

To send an email, you need to know the email address of the person you're writing to – just as you need to know someone's house address to send them a letter.

Email addresses

An email address looks something like this:

myname@myemail.com

The first part says which person the email is for.

The '@' symbol is pronounced 'at'.

The last part is the computer address, called the domain.

DO IT!

Once you've opened up your email program, look for an option called 'New message' or 'Create email'. Fill in the To and Subject fields, and make sure you've got the email address right. If it's not exactly correct, your message won't go to the right person. Click the 'Send' button when you've finished typing in your message.

Email addresses

You put the email address of the person you're writing to in the box marked 'To'.

What's it about?

There's a space for you to explain the subject of your email. This is what it's about – put something short and clear, like 'Party invitation' or 'Homework question'.

To: flossie3@highgroveschool.com

Subject: My party

Hi Flossie -
I'm having a party next Saturday (14th) and I'd love you to come.
It will be at 2-5 pm at my house.
Bye!
Alice

Often, people won't open an email if they don't know what it's about, especially if they don't know who it's from, so remember to fill this in.

Say something!

You don't have to be as formal in an email as a letter, but it's still polite to start with a greeting – maybe 'Dear George' or even 'Hi – how are you?' if it's someone you know well.

At the end of your message, don't forget to put a polite closing remark and your name.

You've got mail!

So you know how to send a message, but what about how to receive one? If you send email messages to people, sooner or later someone will reply to you.

Getting a reply

You'll need to open your mailbox or inbox and then click on the new message to read it. There will be some way of telling the message is new. It might be shown in bold, or have a special picture next to it.

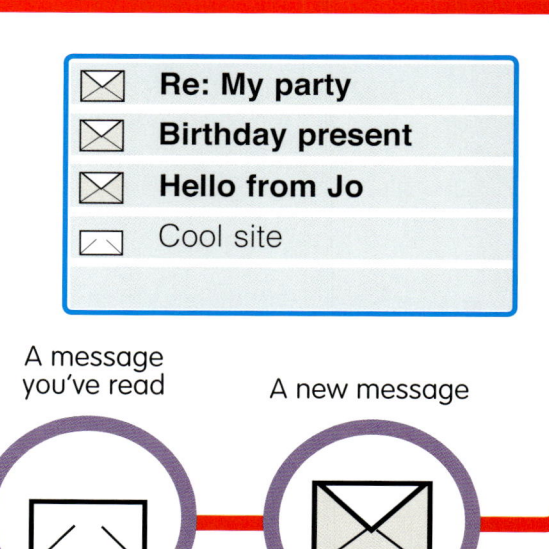

Re: My party
Birthday present
Hello from Jo
Cool site

A message you've read

A new message

Your computer might make a noise to let you know a new message has arrived.

Bling!

Hey! New messages

PRINT IT OUT

It can be useful to print out some of your email messages. You might want to use information in a message away from the computer, or let someone else use the computer. But don't print out all your email!

Your turn

Often, you need to send replies to email messages sent to you. Someone might ask you a question, or you may just be having a chat with them.

There will be a Reply button you can click. This starts a new email, with the right address filled in already. Usually, the other person's message is included, too. Type your own message and click on Send.

To: frankieb@snailmail.com

Subject: RE: my new story

Hi Frankie - good to hear from you
------Original Message-----
From: Frankie Baker [mail to:frankieb@snailmail.com]
Sent: 03 February 2004 10:25
To: Zeb
Subject: my new story

Hello Zeb
Do you remember you said you'd help me with my story?
Yes, of course I'll help - it will be fun.

This is my idea. Please let me know what you think. It is about a boy and his dog. They think a ghost lives in the shed in their garden

Have your say

Sometimes you might want to add comments, or make changes to what the original email says. If you put your comments in a different style, such as bold, that will help the person who sent you the message to see which are your bits.

43

The address book

Email addresses aren't always very easy to remember, but if you get them wrong, your message won't get through. To help you, the computer keeps an **address book** for you.

Keep a list

In the address book, you can keep the email addresses of everyone you want to send messages to. It lists email addresses beside names, as shown below.

Make sure you type the email address in carefully when you put it in the address book.

DO IT!

You might need to open your address book before you can add a name. Look for an option to 'Add name' or 'Add contact'.

Add name

Address Book

Name	Email address
Alex	alex@7delaneyxy.co.uk
Gemma	gemmatan@adxserve.com
Grandma	aclayden@goonline.com
Jody	jody@theclayhouse.co.uk
Stephen	stephen@abxserve.com
Tariq	tkabdul229@goonline.com

44

I must email Grandma

Sending a message

When you want to send a message to someone in your address book, you just need to choose their name from the list and the computer will fill in the address in the 'To' space for you.

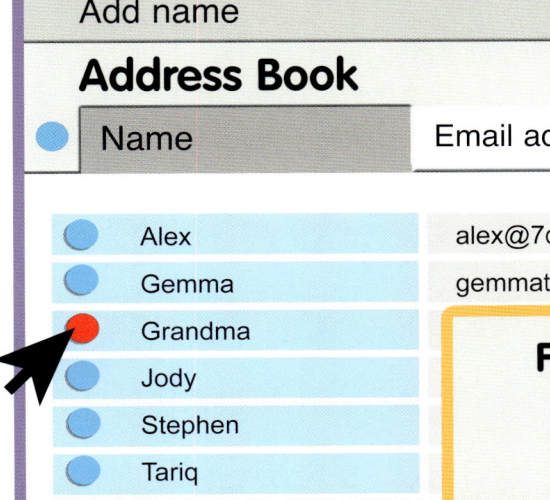

Address Book

Add name

Name	Email address
Alex	alex@7delaneyxy.co.uk
Gemma	gemmatan@adxserve.com
Grandma	
Jody	
Stephen	
Tariq	

From: leanne@bananamail.com
To: aclayden@goonline.com
Subject: Summer holidays

Hello Grandma
How are you? - We were wondering if we could come and visit in the summer holidays?
Dad says we'll be able to come anytime in August...

DO IT!

When you want to use an address, you may be able to click on the 'To' button to see the list, or you might have to open the address book first and pick the person you want to write to.

Attachments

Sometimes words aren't enough, and you need to send something else with your email message. You can add a picture, a document you've written or even a sound file.

Sending extras

An email message is usually just plain words. If you want to show someone some work you've done, or perhaps send them a picture you've made, you can send another computer file along with your message. This is called an `attachment` or enclosure.

It's a bit like putting something else in an envelope along with a letter – like a photo or a drawing, for example.

DO IT!

Look for a button with a picture of a paper clip, or an option to 'Attach File'. You'll need to show the computer where on the computer disk the file is that you want to send, then click on Attach or OK to use it.

Attach file

From: Caitlin@snailmail.com

To: alexb@junioremail.com

Getting attachments

If someone else sends you an email message with an attachment, you'll need to save the attachment and then open it. You'll need the right kind of computer program to open the attachment – so if they've sent you a picture, you'll need an art program.

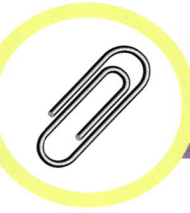

📎 ✉ **Re: My party**
✉ **Birthday present**
✉ **Hello from Jo**
📎 ✉ My fish picture

From: Caitlin@snailmail.com
To: alexb@junioremail.com
Subject: My seahorse picture

Hello Alex
Here is my picture for our fish project.
Love Caitlin

sea horse.bmp

Take care

When you get an email with an attachment, there's usually a picture of a paper clip beside the message. If you get an attachment you're not expecting, or from someone you don't know, ask a grown-up before you open it.

DO IT!

Look for an option to save the attachment. You'll have to tell the computer where to keep it.

Share the message

You can make your own multimedia project with a special program such as PowerPoint, or by making a web page. Sometimes you can even do it in a word-processing program.

On the Web

Building a multimedia web page, or putting a multimedia presentation on a website, is a good way to share something online that's more exciting than just words.

You won't find out here how to put your multimedia work on an online website – that's something your teacher can do for you when you've finished building it. But you could send it as an email attachment to your friends!

Using multimedia

If you've used multimedia CD-ROMs and websites before, you'll know how they work. As well as the words and pictures on the screen, there are buttons or linked words that you can click on to go to more information, or to play a sound or video. Whether it's a word, a button or a picture that's linked, it's called a hotspot or hyperlink. The whole system of linked pages is called hypertext.

Life cycle of a butterfly

Butterfly — A female butterfly lays her eggs on a plant.

Eggs — The eggs hatch out after a few weeks, into caterpillars.

Caterpillar — The caterpillars feed on the plant and grow bigger and bigger.

Chrysalis — Each caterpillar forms a case around itself. Inside, it changes into a butterfly.

Click on a picture in the life cycle to find out more.

Planning multimedia

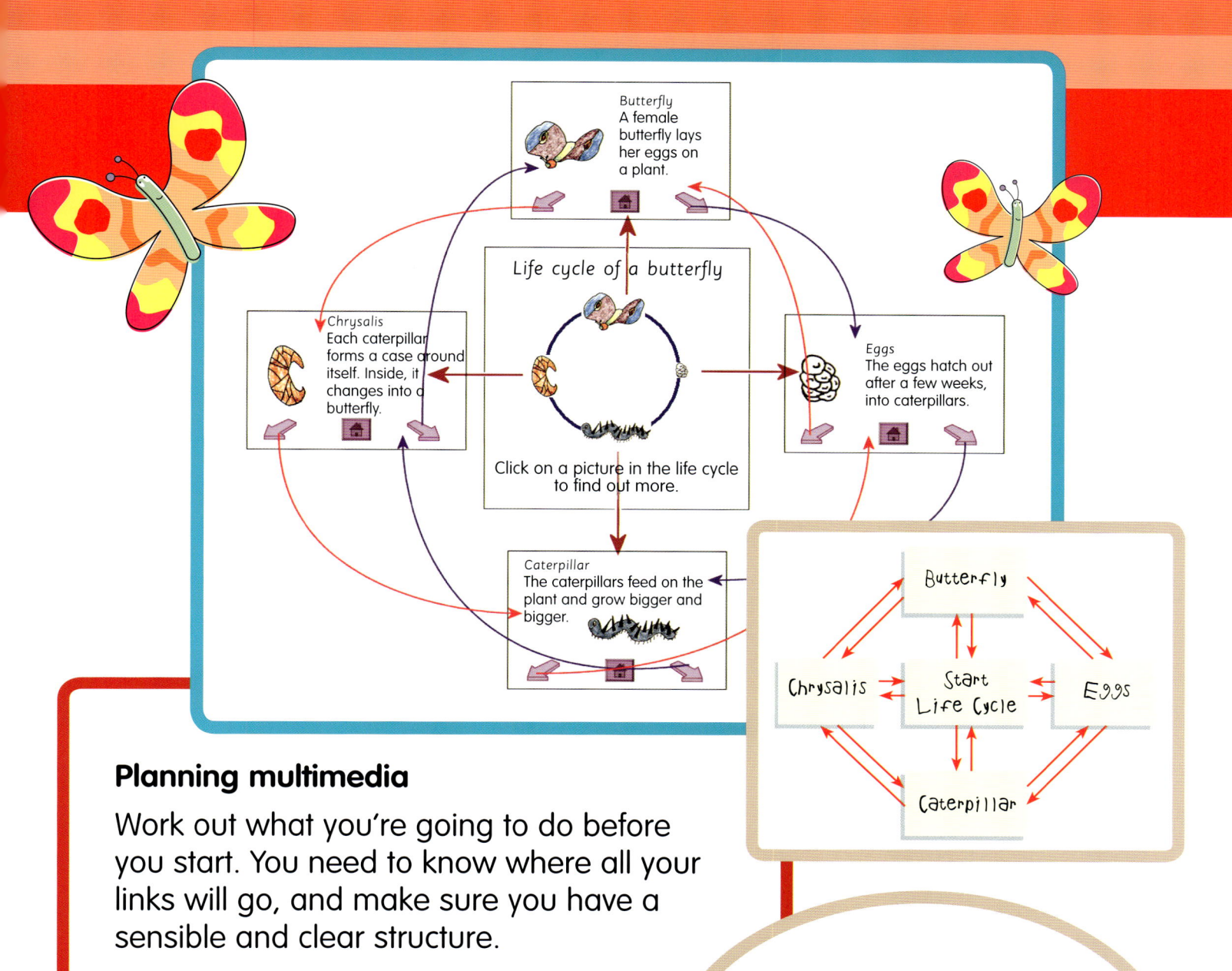

Work out what you're going to do before you start. You need to know where all your links will go, and make sure you have a sensible and clear structure.

It's a good idea to draw a flowchart to show where each link will go.

You'll need to work out how your pages are linked, which pictures and sounds to use and how to make sure people can get back to the start.

DO IT!

Find out how to create new pages in the multimedia program you're using. Look for an option like 'New page' or 'New file'.

You'll need to create each page, add the pictures and words, and then link them together.

49

Looking good

Take a look at some of the multimedia you use yourself and some of the web pages that you like. Try to see how the design of the pages helps you to understand and use a website or CD-ROM.

Design tips

In the best multimedia and web pages, you'll find:

The pages are consistent – they use the same types of headings, the same colours, and items that appear on more than one page are in the same place.

The Tune Bugs

3-piece pop band

News
Gigs
MP3s
Band bio
Pop pics

Contact   Links

The Tune Bugs
Pop pics

Susie   Josh   Jenna

Home   Contact   Links

All the buttons are of a similar design.

They have an area for any buttons that are used a lot, like a button to go back a page, or 'Contact' link.

If little pictures (icons) are used to show choices, it's obvious what they mean.

Your own designs

Sticking to a consistent design is important as it helps people feel at ease with your pages. They quickly learn how to use them and where to look.

Make sure the colours are suitable and the screen is easy to read. Headings should be big enough to stand out and pictures easy to see.

This is hard to read and the size of the words is confusing.

Spotting sharks

The shark looks like this from underneath:

And like this from the side:

This is much clearer.

Spotting sharks

The shark looks like this from underneath:

And like this from the side:

Who's it for?

Think about the people who will be using your presentation. You need to make sure both the design and the words suit your *audience*. So if you're making a multimedia guide to the school for new children in the reception class, it will have to be all pictures. But if you're presenting the results of your science investigation to your class, it can be more complicated.

DO IT!

Find out how to set the background colour for your pages, and how to change the style, colour and size of the words. You might be able to choose a pattern or picture for your background – but make sure the words will show up if you do this.

Make a sound

Most multimedia has some sound. You can record sounds, such as your own speech or singing – or you can make sounds using the computer.

Sound sequences

If you have a music program, you can build up a sound *sequence* on the computer that you can use in your multimedia show or web pages.

Usually, you need to click on a button to play a note or series of notes. Click on several buttons in turn to build up a musical sequence. Find out how to save your sequence so that you can use it in your multimedia work or web page.

When you put music in your multimedia, you should choose or make something suitable – don't use a sad piece of music in a page about parties or weddings!

Recording sound

Many computers have a microphone that you can use to record speech or other sounds. Speak clearly, or make your other sound clearly, and be careful to avoid background noise, such as other people talking, or chairs scraping on the floor.

Play back your sound and check it's all right. If not, record it again.

Extra sounds

You might be able to find sounds that you can use on the World Wide Web or a CD-ROM. For example, you could find animal noises, or sound effects such as wind or thunder. Ask for help from a grown-up if you're going to look on the Web for sounds.

Adding sound and pictures

The point of multimedia presentations is that they contain different kinds of information, such as sounds and pictures.

DIY or ready-made?

Just as you can make your own sounds or get them from the Web or a CD-ROM, so you can draw your own pictures or use ready-made pictures. Make your own using an art program on the computer, or draw them on paper and scan them in with a scanner. Ready-made pictures are often called clip art. You can copy sounds and clip art from CD-ROMs or from the Web.

Where do they go?

A picture can go straight onto your multimedia page. You'll need to link a sound to a button, picture or word so that people can play the sound when they want to by clicking on the link. Make sure it's clear what the button does. You might put a picture on the button, or put a label explaining what to do.

listen to the sound of thunder

54

Types of file

When you want to add pictures and sounds to your multimedia pages, you'll need to make sure you save them as the right type of file, so find out what you need.

Check it!

Don't forget to check that your pages look good, have no mistakes and all the links work properly.

DO IT!

Look for an option to 'Import Picture' or 'Insert Picture'. You will have to tell the computer which picture file to use. You might need to move the picture, or change its size, once you've put it on the page. If you're using a multimedia program, you can change the size by dragging one of the 'handles' on the corners of the picture, or move the picture around the page by dragging it.

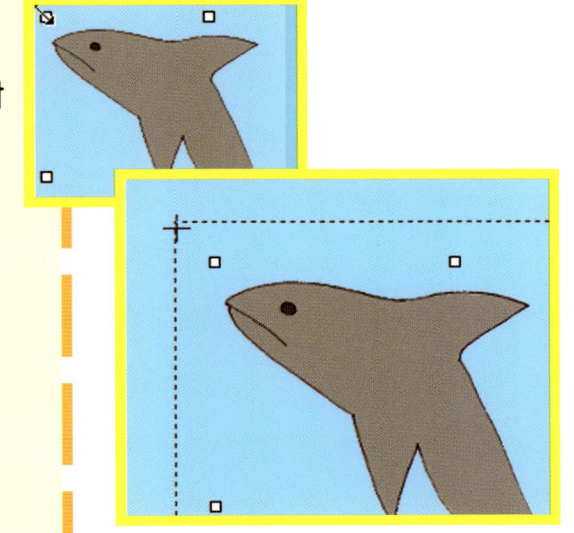

When you add a sound, you might have to choose a button, picture or word then add a sound to it, or add a link and choose your sound file as the linked file.

Finished!

When you've finished, save your work. If you're going to put it on a website, look for an option to 'Save as web page' or 'Save as HTML'. You'll need to keep all the pages and pictures together so that it all still works on the Web.

WRITING PROGRAMS

What's it all about?

All around you, computers and other machines are hard at work, doing all kinds of different jobs. But how do they know what to do? It's all down to the instructions we put into them.

Machines at home

Your house is probably full of equipment that follows instructions – like your remote control TV, microwave oven and programmable washing machine.

But there's plenty more. Some types of equipment watch for changes or events, and then carry out an action. The heating starts up when the temperature drops, and the light in the fridge comes on when you open the fridge door. These are examples of **control technology**, and they work using a **control sequence**.

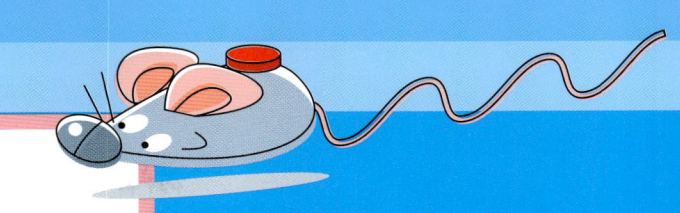

Responding to events

You can spot a control sequence by looking out for anything that responds to some kind of event by carrying out instructions that make something happen.

The event could be information you give or an action you take, such as pressing the buttons on the microwave oven or turning a switch.

Or it could be information the equipment gains from the environment around it, like the temperature, the amount of light or whether anything is moving.

Time to take control!

In this book, you'll find out how control sequences work, and how to use a set of instructions to make something happen. You'll also look at ways of making things happen if something else happens – like making a light come on when it gets dark.

How does it work?

When you go to the supermarket, you tread on a special mat on the floor and the door opens for you. This is an example of a control sequence. Let's take a closer look at how it works...

Input and output

In the supermarket door control sequence, the event that makes the door open is your weight on the mat. This is called the **input** to the system.

The instructions tell the door 'if someone stands on the mat, open the door'.

The door opening is the result – it's called the **output**.

Input

Output

60

Input

Output

More inputs and outputs

Types of input include things such as changes in temperature, the amount of humidity (water in the air) and certain types of movement – or more obvious events like someone pressing a button.

Types of output are things such as moving an object, making a sound or turning a light on or off. In some cars, the windscreen wipers turn on if the windscreen senses rain. Rain is the input; moving the wipers is the output.

Get it right

Let's go back to the supermarket. The instruction 'if someone stands on the mat, open the door' is not quite as simple as it looks. The door must open if something heavy enough to be a person treads on the mat. But the door shouldn't open if a bee lands on it, or a bit of rubbish blows onto it.

And how heavy is a person? Should the door open if a light person – a child – treads on the mat? Maybe not at the exit, or small children might be able to run away.

61

What do you want to do?

A set of instructions to control something can be called a control sequence or a **program**. Writing instructions is called **programming.**

Turtle technology

If you work on control technology at school, you'll probably start by working with a floor turtle or tortoise. It's a simple robot that moves around on the floor according to the instructions – or programs – that you give it.

You might also use computer software that works in the same way, following your instructions to draw lines or patterns on the screen.

Think first

Before you start giving instructions, think about what you want to achieve! That might sound obvious, but remember that any computer or electrical device can only do exactly what you tell it. It can't make any decisions for itself.

So you can't just say 'turn the heating on if it gets cold' – you have to decide exactly what temperature counts as 'cold'.

Once you've worked out what you want (the output) and what is going to make it happen (the input), you can write the instructions.

10°C

19°C

Using sensors

Many control systems, like the supermarket door, act on information from their surroundings. They have **sensors** – devices that can detect things like light, pressure or temperature.

If you want a light to come on when it gets dark, for example, you'll need an electrical circuit with a light sensor that can sense light levels. This type of system **monitors** the environment – it keeps checking whether it's dark and turns the light on if it is.

Hmm! It's getting darker...

Dark enough – time to switch on!

63

Writing instructions

Now let's have a look at how you can give instructions to a floor turtle to make it follow a particular route.

Lettuce quest

Imagine you wanted to move the turtle from where it is to the lettuce.

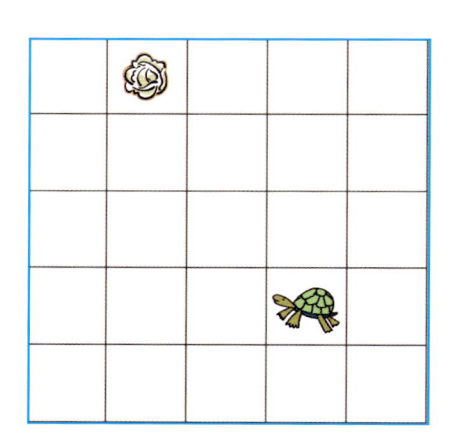

The turtle can only go up, down, left or right. To get there quickly, it could go:

- Up three squares, then left two

or

- Left two squares, then up three

Tell the turtle

To make a floor turtle or tortoise do something like this, you need to use the buttons on it to give it the right instructions. To take the second route, for example, you'd need to press these buttons:

Forward 2 — 'Forward 2' tells the turtle to go forward two spaces.

Right 90 — 'Right 90' tells it to turn 90 degrees to the right.

Forward 3 — 'Forward 3' tells it to go forward another three spaces.

Go — The 'Go' button tells the turtle the instructions are finished, and it can start to carry them out.

64

On the screen

Instead of a floor turtle, you might use a computer program such as **Logo** to draw a route on the screen. This will have extra instructions, such as 'Pendown' (start drawing lines) and 'Penup' (stop drawing).

These instructions draw a square:

Pendown
Forward 4
Right 90
Forward 4
Right 90
Forward 4
Right 90
Forward 4
Penup

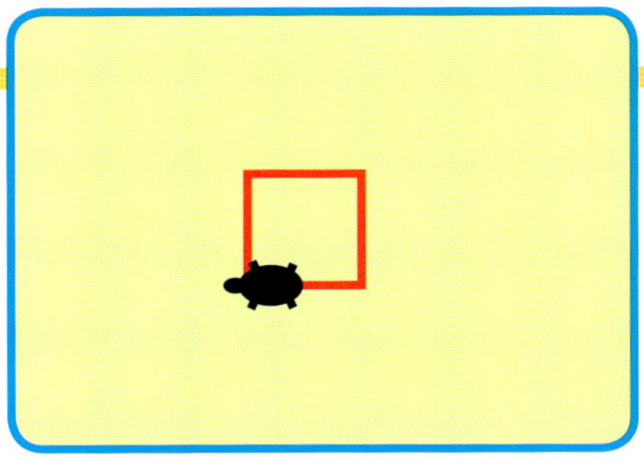

Leave a space

If you move the screen turtle or pen after a 'penup' instruction, a line is not drawn. You can use this to leave a space before doing the next bit of your drawing. For example, this program draws a line, leaves a space, and draws another line.

Pendown
Forward 2
Penup
Forward 1
Pendown
Forward 2
Penup

65

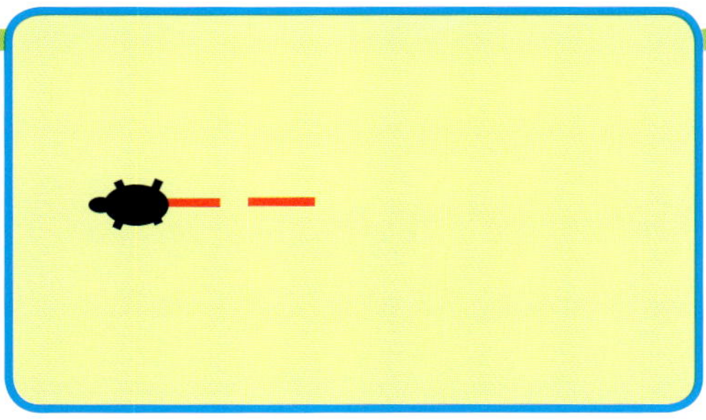

Do it again!

You'll often want to use the same instructions again and again. You don't need to type in the same instructions lots of times, though – you can tell the screen turtle to repeat an instruction.

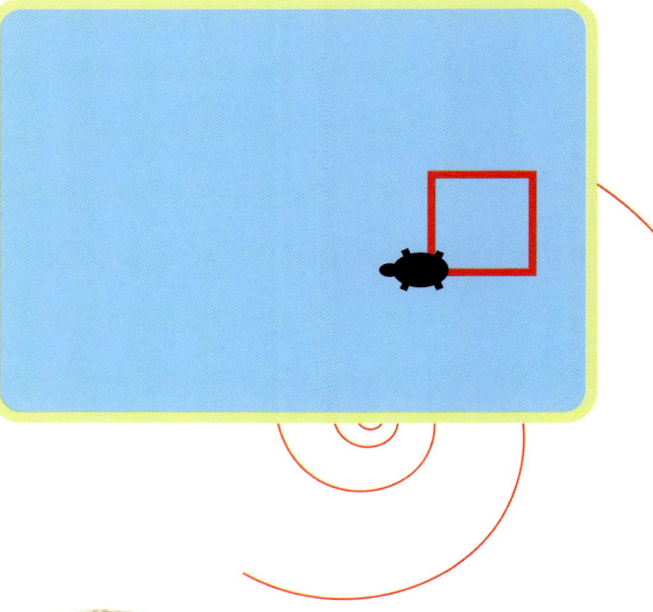

Make a loop

To draw a square, you can use the same instruction several times. This is called a **loop** or a **repeat**. So instead of the sequence shown on page 17, you could write:

Pendown
Repeat 3
[Forward 4
Right 90]
Forward 4
Penup

This tells the computer to repeat the instructions 'Forward 4, Right 90' three times, then draw a final line to complete the square.

Give it a name

If you want to use the same set of instructions again and again, you can give it a name. When you've done this, you can use it just by typing its name.

A set of instructions with a name is called a **procedure**. If we called the procedure to draw a square 'square', we could then draw lots of squares with spaces in between them, like this:

Square
Forward 2
Square
Forward 2
Square

Remember that the 'penup' instruction at the end of the square procedure means no line is drawn until the next 'pendown'.

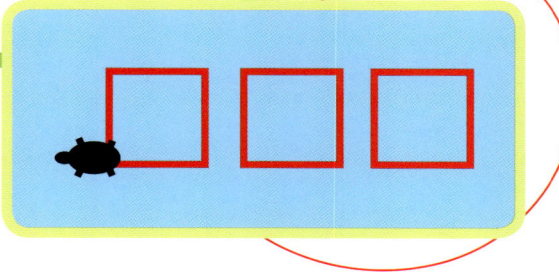

DO IT!

There are different versions of Logo and other similar programs, so you'll have to find out the exact instructions yours uses. Find out which type of brackets you need to use – it might be (and) or [and].

67

Make a pattern

If you can repeat shapes, and you can leave spaces between them or turn the pen or turtle around between them, you can easily draw patterns.

Drawing shapes

So far, you've drawn squares and lines. Here are some more shapes to try:

Rectangle

You can draw a rectangle by drawing two long sides and two short sides:

Pendown
Repeat 2
[Forward 4
Right 90
Forward 2
Right 90]
Penup

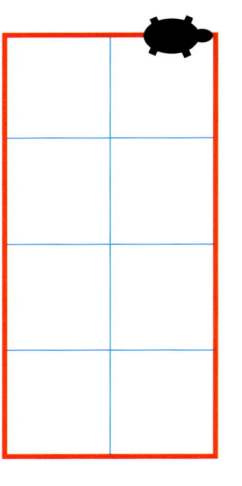

Triangle

You can draw a triangle by changing the angles the turtle turns at:

Pendown
Repeat 3
[Forward 8
Right 120]
Penup

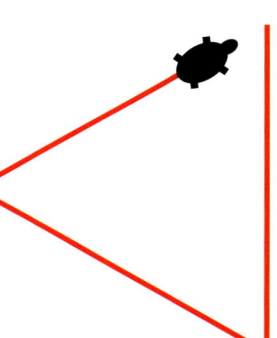

Remember that your turtle is turning around the outside of each corner of the triangle.

68

Mystery shape

Can you work out from reading the program what this shape will look like?

```
Pendown
Repeat 360
[Forward 1
Right 1]
Penup
```

Make a windmill

You can draw a windmill by repeating a triangle four times, turning 90 degrees each time.

You'd start by writing a procedure to draw a triangle, then use it with a 90 degree turn, repeating four times:

```
Pendown
Repeat 4
[Triangle
Right 90]
Penup
```

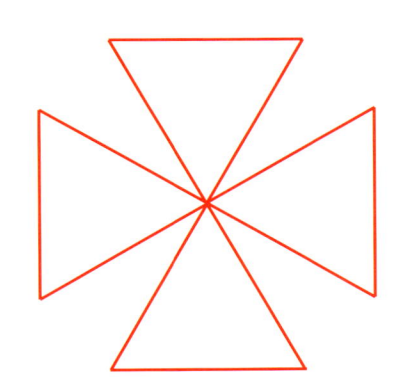

It's snowing!

If you use 'penup' to stop drawing while you move the pen or turtle, you can draw a shape like this:

You could save this as a procedure called 'snowflake' and then draw it six times to make a snowflake:

Testing, testing

Drawing more complicated shapes can be tricky, and you might make a few mistakes to start with. Don't worry – this happens even to people who write computer programs for a living! Always test your programs to avoid problems.

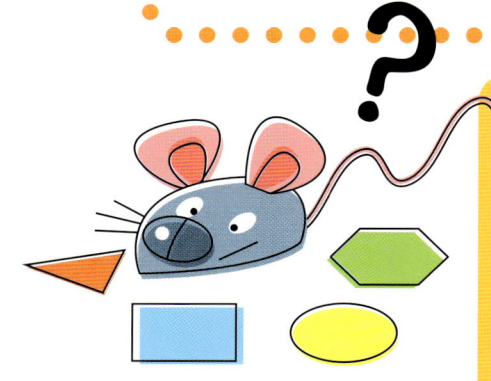

Step by step

All sets of instructions need to be tested to make sure they work. And if you're using loops or procedures, it's best to try out each step to make sure it works before you go any further.

Separate parts

Suppose you wanted to draw a row of houses, like this:

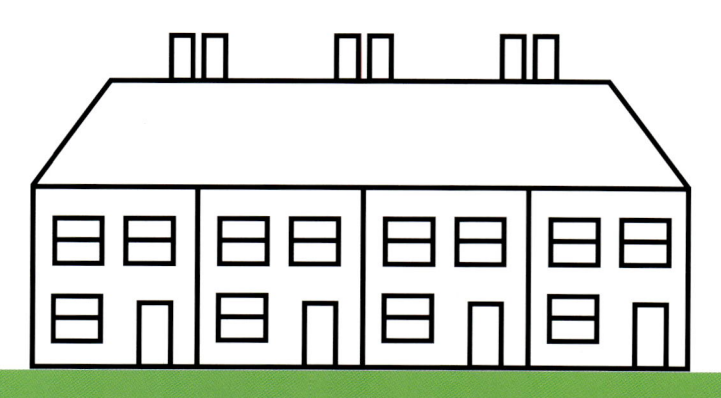

You would write procedures to draw the chimneys, windows and doors as different types of box. Try out all the procedures separately, before writing the whole set of instructions, to make sure they work.

Looking for mistakes

If your instructions don't work, either nothing will happen, or the wrong thing will happen. You'll need to find out why. There might be a message telling you where the instructions have gone wrong, which will help you find the mistake.

Look for:

- **Spelling mistakes**

  If you've used the wrong word, missed out a space or spelled a word wrongly, your instructions won't work.

  What's a squarw?

- **Wrong numbers**

  If you move the pen the wrong number of spaces or turn through the wrong angle, it won't draw the shape you want.

- **Missing something out**

  If you miss something out – like a turn, a number, a bracket or a procedure – you won't get what you expect.

Ask a friend to check your program to see if they can spot any problems.

Planning a sequence

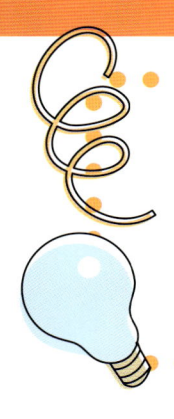

In everyday life, you're surrounded by devices that are part of control sequences. They all follow lists of instructions and procedures.

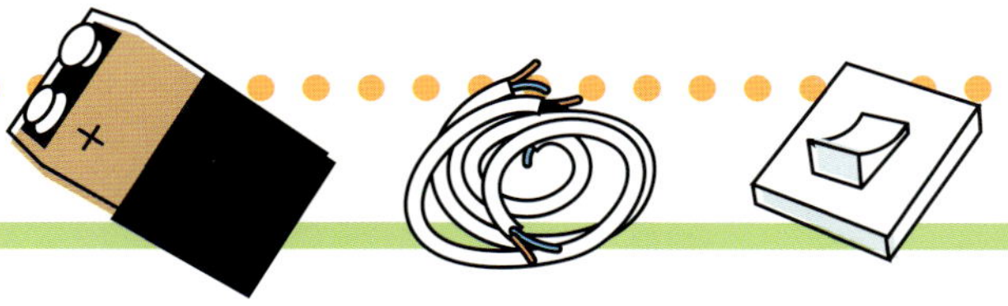

Plan it

When programmers write instructions to make a sequence work, they have to plan carefully. Before programming a set of traffic lights, they'd ask:

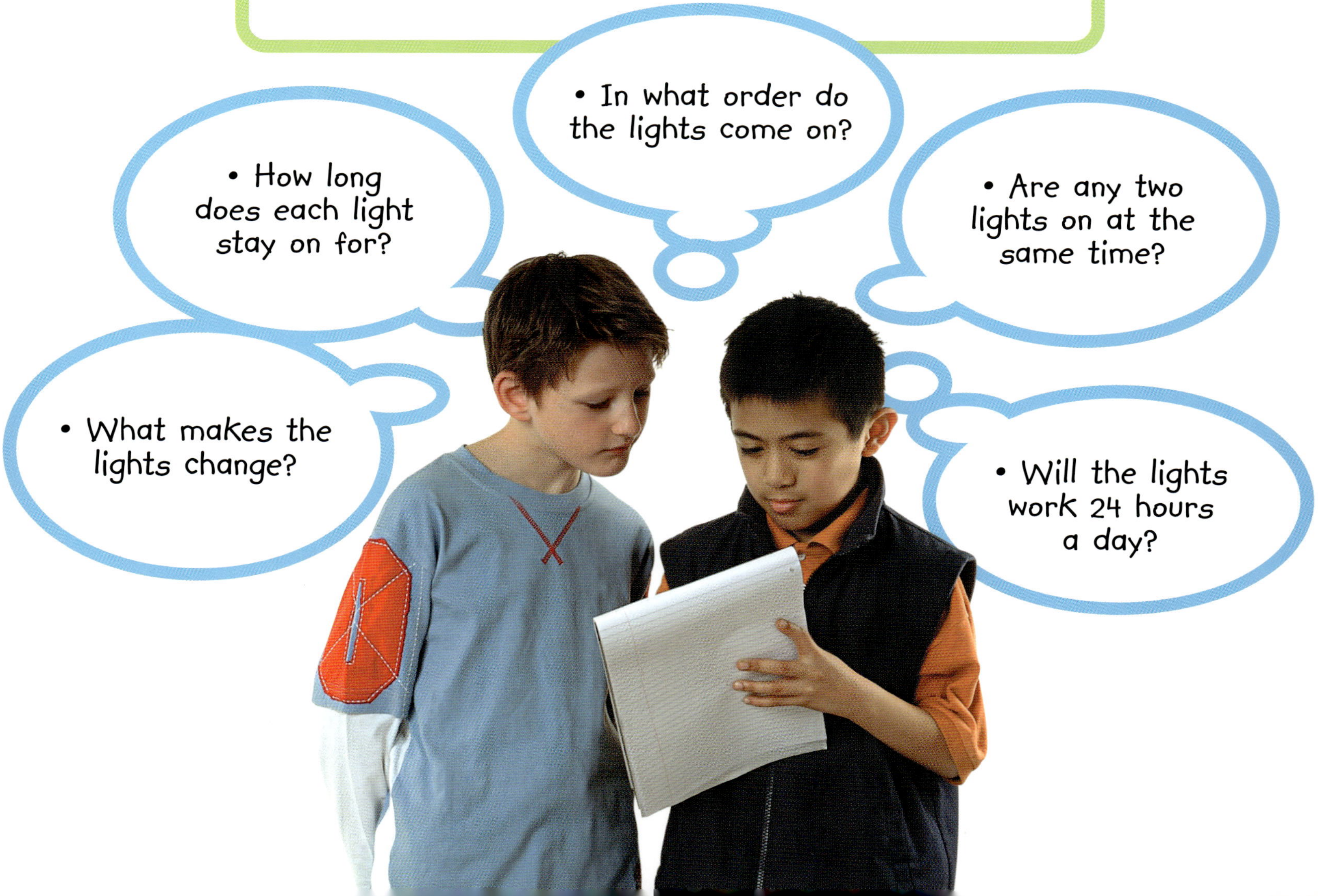

- In what order do the lights come on?
- How long does each light stay on for?
- Are any two lights on at the same time?
- What makes the lights change?
- Will the lights work 24 hours a day?

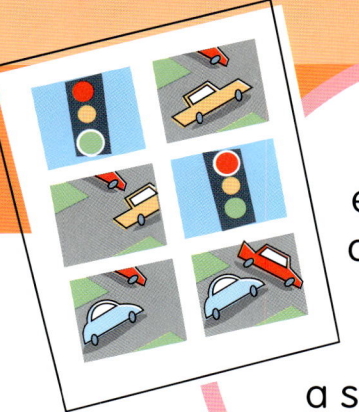

It's often easiest to plan a control sequence by drawing a storyboard – a set of drawings that show all the different stages.

DO IT!

Try drawing your own storyboard showing a sequence of traffic lights coming on in different combinations. Think about how you could write a program to make this happen.

Perfect timing

Many control sequences work on time intervals. The traffic lights have to be set to stay red or green a sensible length of time, and the timing in the instructions needs to be carefully matched to the traffic patterns.

If you've got a simple control box and some electrical components, you could even try making a set of working lights.

Often, the timing on traffic lights changes during the day, so that traffic going into town gets more time in the morning, and traffic coming out gets more time in the evening when everyone is going home. Getting it wrong will cause people to become cross and impatient, and could even lead to accidents.

Triggering events

Control technologies work by using an input to **trigger** an event, or make something happen. The input can come from a person, or it can be detected automatically.

Switches and sensors

A system operated by a switch works when someone presses the switch – so, for example, a pedestrian light changes when a person presses the button. If no one wants to cross the road, the lights don't change.

Other systems use sensors to decide when to work. A sensor detects changes – such as differences in light, noise or pressure.

So:

An alarm in an art gallery might go off if a light beam is broken by someone leaning too close to a picture.

A sprinkler comes on if it senses smoke.

An automatic cat flap opens when it senses signals from a transmitter on the cat's collar.

Monitoring changes

Some sensors monitor changes in the environment. You could use a thermometer as a sensor to see how the temperature changes over the day or year.

Sometimes, sensors are connected to computers so that the computer can take readings automatically at regular intervals.

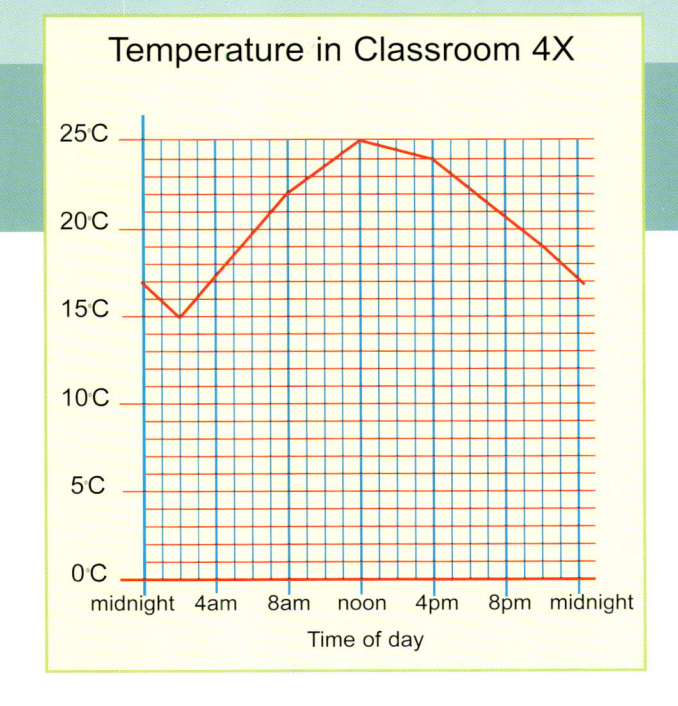

Temperature in Classroom 4X

Connecting a sensor to a computer means you can make readings without having to be there all the time. For example, you could measure the temperature at school all night long.

DO IT!

Find out how to link a sensor to a computer. Make sure you know how to set the interval for monitoring and how to read the recordings. Then monitor the temperature, light level or sound level over a day and a night.

1 JULY – gets dark at 9.20pm

1 SEPTEMBER – gets dark at 7.30pm

1 DECEMBER – gets dark at 3.55pm

Making it happen

With a sensor connected to a control system, we can make things happen when a certain event or condition happens. So street lights come on when it gets dark enough. They can't be set on a timer, as it gets dark at different times throughout the year.

On and on and on...

In real life, control technology systems keep working 24 hours a day. They are constantly checking the input, so that they can give the right output.

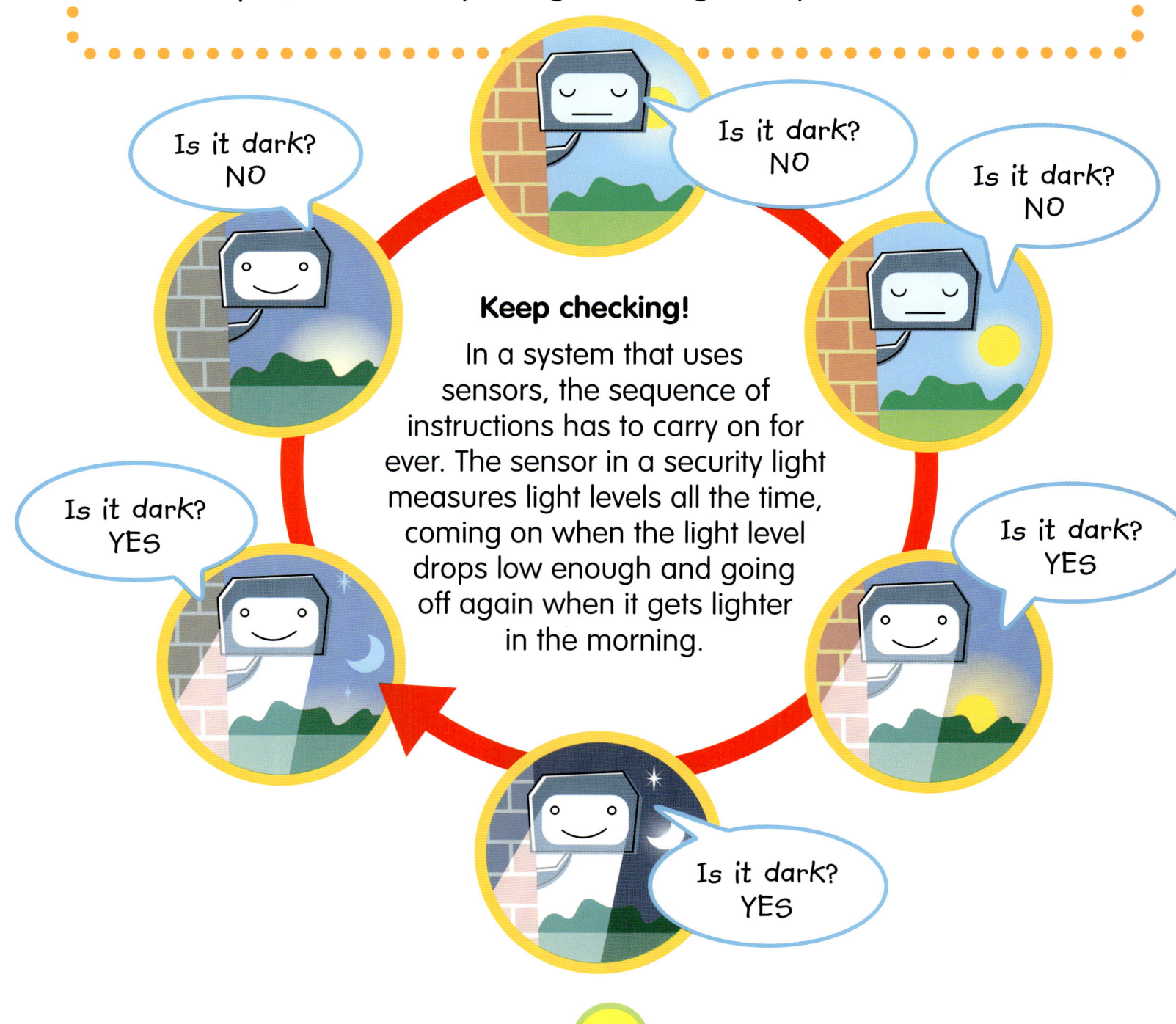

Is it dark? NO

Is it dark? NO

Is it dark? NO

Is it dark? YES

Is it dark? YES

Is it dark? YES

Keep checking!

In a system that uses sensors, the sequence of instructions has to carry on for ever. The sensor in a security light measures light levels all the time, coming on when the light level drops low enough and going off again when it gets lighter in the morning.

When and what?

When designing a system that uses sensors, you need to decide:

- How often you want your system to check the sensors.

- The level of reading that will trigger an event.

Regular checks

Some systems don't have to be checked very often. A central heating system could check the temperature in the room every ten or fifteen minutes.

Others need to be more sensitive. A life support system in a hospital, that sounds a buzzer if a patient's heart stops, has to check every few seconds.

What's the trigger?

The system can't decide what you would count as dark or quiet or heavy – you need to pick a level. The central heating could be set to turn on the heating if the temperature falls below, say, 20°C. The life support system could be set to go off if there is no heartbeat for more than three seconds.

Perfect!

You need to test your instructions while you're working on them, and when you've finished, to make sure they do what you set out to do.

Does it work?

As long as you've tested your control sequence step by step as you've built it up, it should all work properly. If not, look for mistakes where you've put the procedures together.

For example, if you end a procedure with 'penup' and don't have a 'pendown' instruction in or before your next procedure, the next one won't draw anything!

Is it what you wanted?

Compare the end result with your original aims. Even if you've followed your plans carefully, you might be able to see a better way. There may be a more direct route for your floor turtle, a simpler procedure to draw the shape you want or a better control sequence.

If your project involves monitoring or sensing, have you chosen the best settings? Is the event triggered at the right time or by the right conditions? Are there any errors in your system?

For example, if you're monitoring temperature, is your sensor sometimes in sunlight and sometimes in shade? If so, move it so that you're always comparing shade temperatures.

Know your limits

It's not always possible to improve the system quite as you'd like. You may be limited by the equipment you have available, or the number of readings you can take.

Even if you can't change these things, it's important that you know what the limits of your system are so that you can work within them.

PICTURES, PHOTOS AND PAINTINGS

What's it all about?

Imagine how boring all the things you read would be without pictures. Pictures liven up the page or screen, grab your interest and even help explain things.

Making pictures

In your own work, you can add pictures by drawing with pencils or pens, or by making pictures on the computer. You can even do a picture partly by hand and partly with the computer by scanning in a picture and then adding to it on screen.

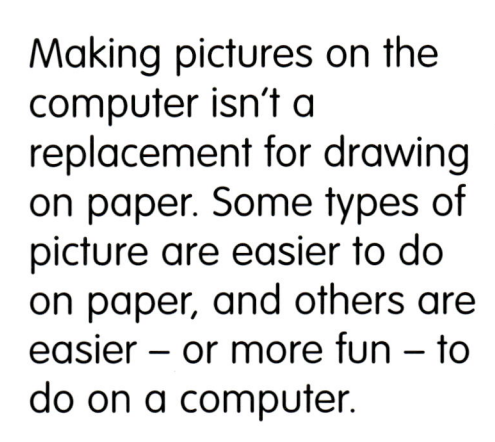

Making pictures on the computer isn't a replacement for drawing on paper. Some types of picture are easier to do on paper, and others are easier – or more fun – to do on a computer.

When do I need a computer?

The computer's great if you want to try out ideas, make a repeating pattern or draw a detailed plan. And if you want pictures to put in a web page or in a presentation you're making on screen, using the computer is the only way.

Pictures made using a computer are sometimes called 'computer graphics'.

This book is all about making pictures on the computer. You'll find out how to make all kinds of pictures, from paintings and drawings to plans, collages and even trick photos.

Think first

When you're making a picture on the computer, think first and plan what you're going to do.

Who, what, why, how?
Ask yourself these questions before you begin:

- **What's my picture for?**
The aim of your picture is called its purpose. For example, it could be to explain an idea, decorate something or illustrate a story.

- **What should it be like?**
Look at lots of pictures to help you decide what you like, and you'll soon learn how pictures work, what is most effective, and why. This is often called developing your 'eye'.

- **Who's going to look at it?**
The people who will look at your picture are called the audience. If you put up a poster, the audience is everyone who walks past. If your picture's in a newsletter, anyone who sees the newsletter is your audience.

- **How are you going to use it?**
Think about how your picture will be used. Is it a logo, an illustration for a story or a picture to put on a card? Plan the type, size and style of the picture to make sure it works.

Types of picture

You can make two very different types of picture on the computer – paintings and drawings. They work in different ways and you can do different things with them.

Paintings

In a painting, you fill in areas of the screen with different colours and patterns.

Drawings

In a drawing, you build up a picture using lines and shapes – sometimes called objects – that can be moved around.

85

Paintings

In a painting program, you make a picture by changing the colour of different areas of the screen.

How painting works

A computer screen is made up of tiny dots of colour, called *pixels*. The computer remembers a painting by keeping track of which colour each pixel has to be.

Colour palette

The colour palette gives you a choice of colours. Click on the colour you want to use – then use your mouse to paint with it.

With a painting program, you can go over any mistakes easily or repaint a whole area if you change your mind.

DO IT!

Open up your painting program and you'll see a blank painting area with a selection of tools and colours. Use your mouse to select the ones you want to use.

When you are using a computer, you don't need to decide on a colour in advance – you can try out lots of different colour schemes.

Toolbox

The tool set or toolbox lets you choose different ways of painting. To choose a tool, just click on it.

Painting tools

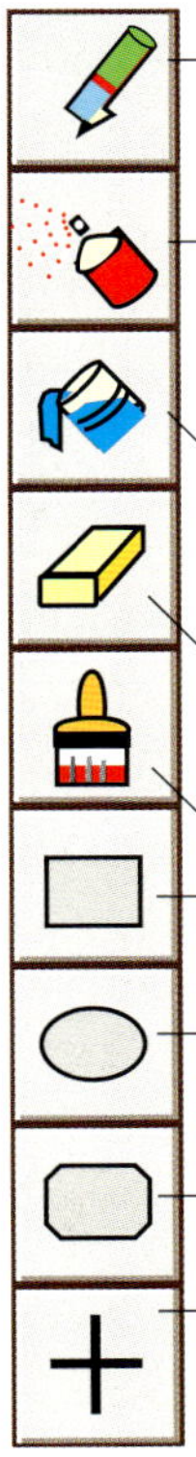

The pencil draws a really thin line.

An airbrush or aerosol can 'sprays' paint on the picture.

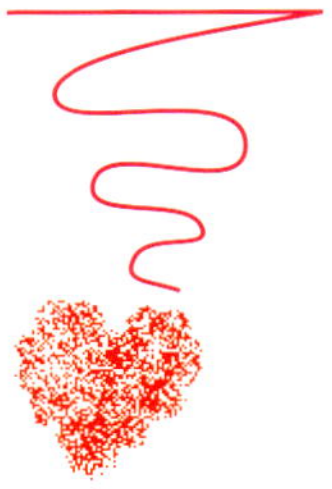

The flood fill tool fills large areas with colour.

The rubber is for rubbing out lines and shapes.

There are usually several brushes for painting lines of different thicknesses.

Other tools make simple shapes and straight lines.

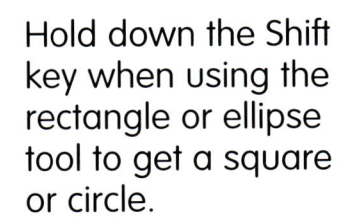

Hold down the Shift key when using the rectangle or ellipse tool to get a square or circle.

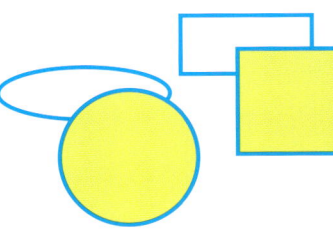

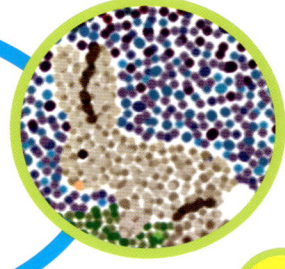

Background colours

When you start, your painting will probably have a white background. You can change it with the flood fill tool. It has a picture of paint pouring out of a pot.

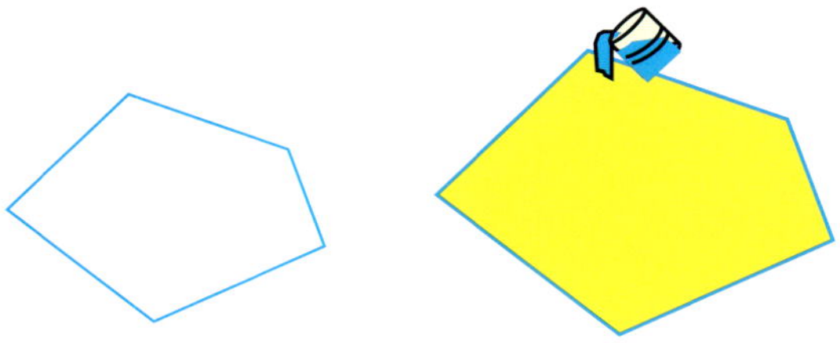

When you've selected the flood fill tool, pick a colour and click on the background to fill the page with it. You can also use it to fill in shapes, and your program may also let you flood fill areas with patterns.

You can use shapes, lines and the flood fill tool to make a Mondrian-style painting.

Make a Pointillist picture by adding spots of colour with a brush.

All change!

It's much easier to make changes to your paintings on the computer than it is on paper.

Moving and copying

You can select (choose) an area of the picture and then move it around, make copies of it or just delete it.

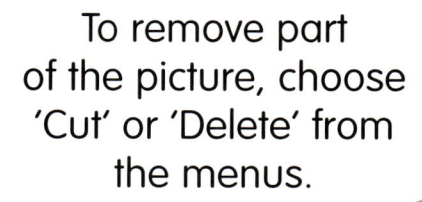

DO IT!

Click the 'select' tool and use the mouse to draw a rectangle over the part of the picture you want to select.

To remove part of the picture, choose 'Cut' or 'Delete' from the menus.

To copy it, choose 'Copy'. Choose 'Paste' to stick the copy you've made somewhere else.

To move an area of your picture, select it and drag it to where you want it.

Multiple copies

You can use 'Paste' to add lots of copies. Paste lots of copies to make a pattern.

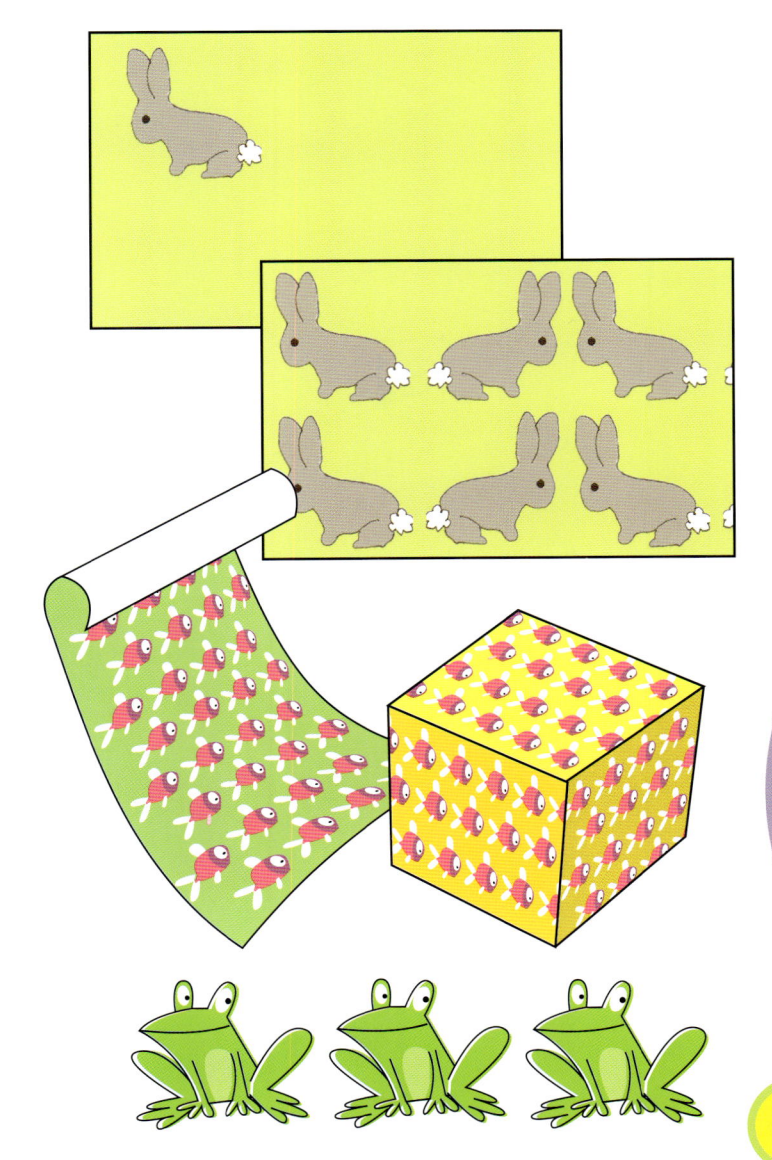

More changes

Look for these options, too, and try them out:

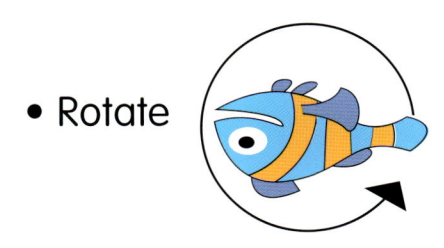

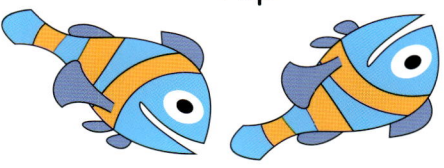

- Rotate

- Flip

- Reflect or Mirror

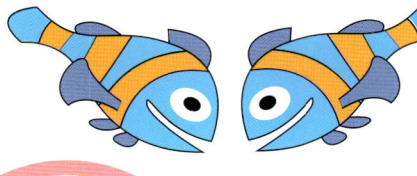

Oops!

If you make a mistake and want to go back, look for an 'Undo' option. Save your painting with a different name every few minutes – then you can go back several stages if you change your mind.

Working with photos

If you have a **digital camera**, you can use photos as the starting point of your painting. With a **scanner**, you can scan photos from paper into the computer to work on them.

Putting photos into your computer

A digital camera takes a photo and stores it on a computer chip instead of on film. You can copy it straight from the camera onto your computer and open it in your painting program.

If you don't have a digital camera, you can use an ordinary photo and scan it into your computer.

DO IT!

Open your photo using your painting program. Then you can add extra bits to it using the paintbrushes and other tools.

Cropping

You can crop a picture to cut it down to just the bit you want to use. You will probably need to select the bit you want to keep and then use a crop tool or option, but check how your program works.

Adding words

To add words to your picture, you have to use a text tool. This lets you type the words and pick the font (style) and size of letters you want. It usually appears in the toolbox as either the letter A or the letter T.

Speech and thought bubbles

To add a speech or thought bubble to a photo (or other picture), first add a shape for the bubble, and then add text on top.

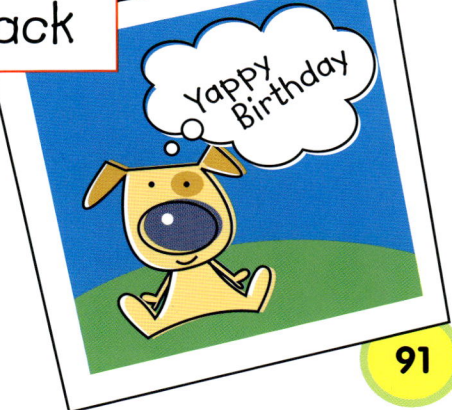

Drawings

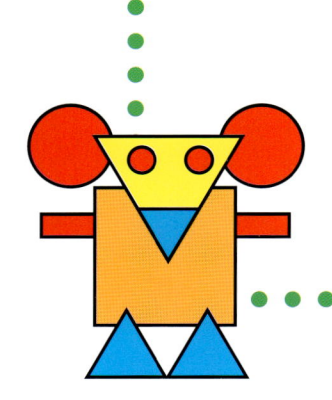

When you use a drawing program to make pictures, the computer remembers your picture by keeping a record of where lines and shapes start and end.

When to draw

If you want to be able to draw accurately and maybe move parts of your picture around, a drawing is often better than a painting.

Objects

A drawing is made up of objects – things like lines and shapes. In a drawing, you can select a line or a box and move it somewhere else. (In a painting, a line or box is just a collection of coloured pixels, so all you can do is select the area it's in.)

In a painting, you can only move whole areas of your picture.

In a drawing, you can move each object by itself.

You need different types of computer programs to make paintings and drawings. However, some word-processors will let you make drawings. If you have a word-processing program, look for a 'Drawing' toolbar or menu option.

92

DO IT!

Look in your drawing program for a toolbox that will let you create different objects – such as boxes, circles, ellipses, straight lines and curved lines. Click on a tool to select it. It may stay selected or you might need to double-click to keep it selected.

Adding words

You can add words to your drawing, too. You can choose the style and colour, and treat them like any other object. This means you can reverse them, stretch them and move them.

Object styles

When you choose a drawing tool, you can often make extra choices – like how thick the lines should be, or whether a shape will be empty inside or filled with colour.

Reflection
Reflection

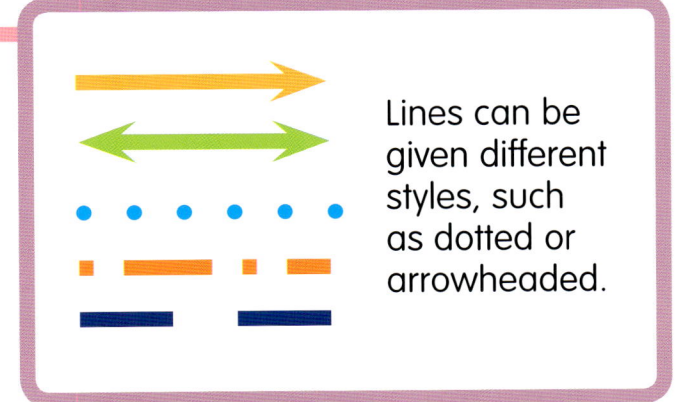

Lines can be given different styles, such as dotted or arrowheaded.

Shapes can be outlines, fills or filled outlines.

93

Making changes

Because each object in a drawing is a separate thing, you can move or change one without changing any other parts of the picture.

DO IT!

To move or change an object, you first have to select it. Look for a tool that looks like an arrow.

Click on the arrow and then on the object you want to select.

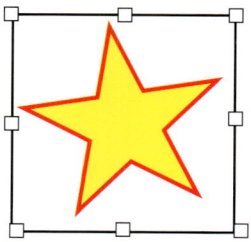

Start making changes

Once you've selected an object you can:

• Move it – just put the mouse over it, hold down the mouse button and drag the object.

• Change the size and shape. Drag a corner handle to make it bigger or smaller while keeping it in proportion.

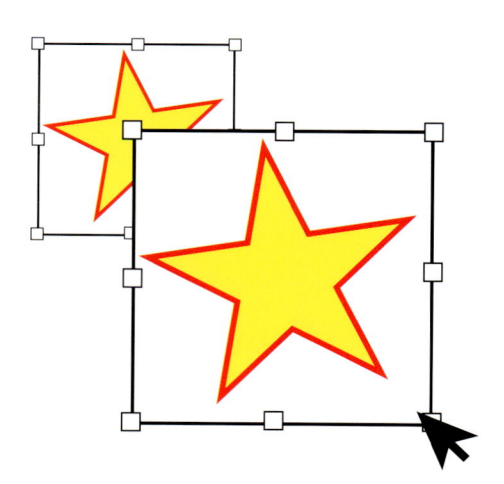

Get a handle on it

When you select an object, little blocks usually appear at the ends, corners or edges. These are called handles.

More changes

- Drag a handle on one side to distort an object, squashing or stretching it.

- Change the colour. If you select an object and then click on a new colour, the colour of the object will change.

Make a pattern

Copy an object and paste it in lots of times to make a repeating pattern.

Make a poster

You can decorate posters with drawings made up of simple shapes. If you need lots of similar things in your picture – like lots of hats – draw one, copy and paste it, and then make changes to the copies.

Pile it up

When you work with a painting program, anything you add over the top of part of your picture replaces what was there before. But with a drawing program, objects can be **layered** one on top of another.

Transparent sheets

Imagine a pile of transparent sheets – like the plastic sheets used for overhead projectors. This is how layering objects works. Each thing you add to the picture in a drawing program is like a new sheet laid on top.

If you put the sheets in a different order, different parts of the picture come to the front.

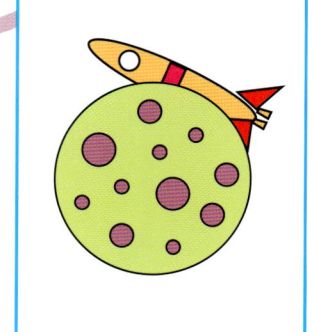

If you take one sheet away, the others stay the same.

96

Order, order!

If your objects overlap or are layered, you might want to rearrange them to make a different pattern or picture, or so that you can see one that's hidden. To do this, you'll need to move the front object aside or send it further down the pile.

This object is at the front.

This object is at the back.

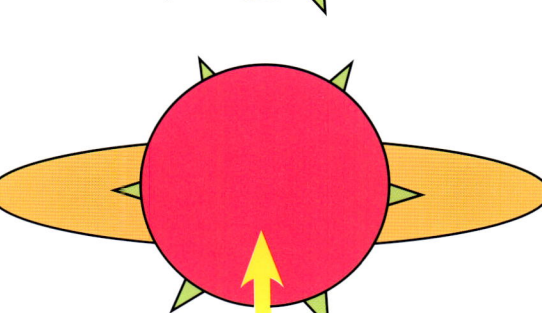

DO IT!
Click on the object in front and look for a menu option called 'Send to back' or 'Move back'. This will send that object to the bottom of the pile.

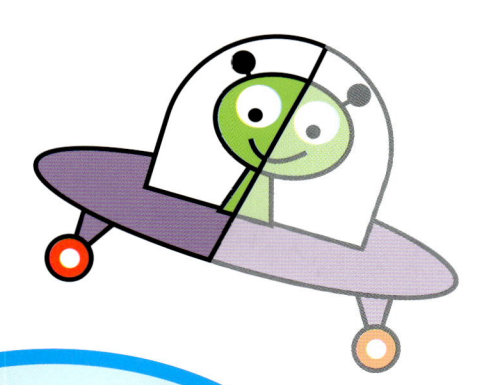

By arranging the objects in a different order, you can make a different pattern.

You might also need to reorder the objects if you want to select one that's at the bottom or middle of the pile.

97

Making plans

A plan is a drawing that helps you design or arrange something. For example, a **plan** of your bedroom would show where your bed is, where the door and window are, and so on.

To scale

The best plans are drawn 'to scale'. This means that the sizes of the things on your plan relate to their real sizes. For example, in a plan of a kitchen, if the table is twice as long as the freezer, then on the plan the table must be twice as long as the freezer too.

To draw a scale plan, you need to decide the scale – that is, the relationship between sizes in the real world and sizes on your plan.

A scale of 1:10 means things are ten times bigger in the real world than in your drawing. So if your kitchen was 2.5 metres long, you'd draw it 25 centimetres long on the plan.

Remember, you can add text to your drawings – so you can put labels and notes on your plans.

On the grid

Most drawing programs have a grid you can make objects 'snap' to. This helps you position objects accurately so that it looks neat.

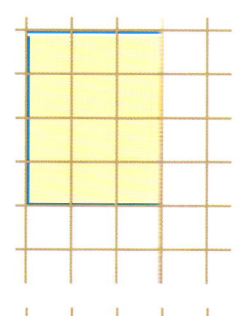

In this picture, the corners of the box are snapping to the grid.

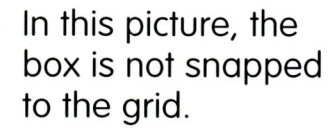

In this picture, the box is not snapped to the grid.

DO IT!

Look for a button or menu option called 'Grid' or 'View grid'. This will display a grid that will help you line up parts of your picture or plan. You should be able to choose whether objects snap to the grid, and you might be able to set the grid spacing.

Gran's garden

Our classroom

Lots of things

Plans often include several copies of the same object. For example, a plan of your classroom would have lots of desks and chairs in it, all the same size as each other. You only need to draw one of each – you can copy and paste to get all the others.

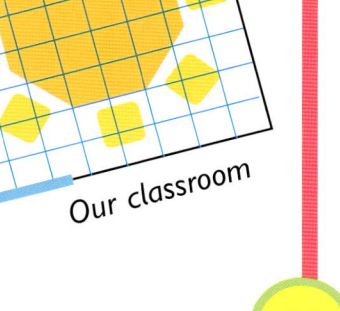

Make a model

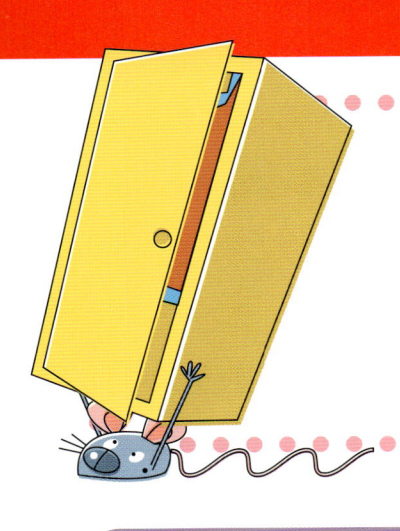

You can use the computer for graphic modelling, too. This sounds really impressive, but it's not hard. A **model** lets you try out different ways of doing something without actually having to do it.

From plan to model

A plan of your room can be used for modelling. You can move the furniture around on your plan to try different arrangements for your room without actually having to shift heavy beds and wardrobes. When you've found an arrangement you like, you can then move the furniture.

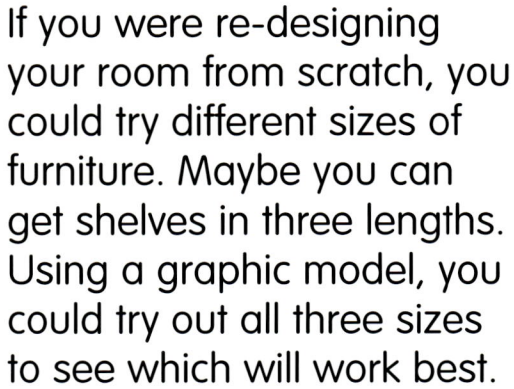

If you were re-designing your room from scratch, you could try different sizes of furniture. Maybe you can get shelves in three lengths. Using a graphic model, you could try out all three sizes to see which will work best.

Designer dreams

Designers work with graphic models all the time. If a designer wants to make up a new car, a new outfit or packaging for a new product, they start with a drawing. If the drawing's on the computer, they can make lots of changes to try out different colours, shapes, sizes and styles.

Version 1

Version 2

Version 3

Wanda's fish food

keep your fish... strong and healthy

Version 1

Wanda's fish food

We're healthy

and strong

Version 2

Before you start experimenting, save a copy of your basic drawing or plan as a template. You can copy it and use it to make lots of designs, then choose the one you like best.

101

Perfect!

Few artists or illustrators get their work totally right first time. Checking and **reviewing** is an important stage in any piece of work.

Take a look

Check your picture on the screen before you print it out on paper. This lets you see if it's too big for the page, if you've missed anything out or if there are any mistakes.

DO IT!

Look for a 'Print Preview' option to see how your picture will look when it's printed.

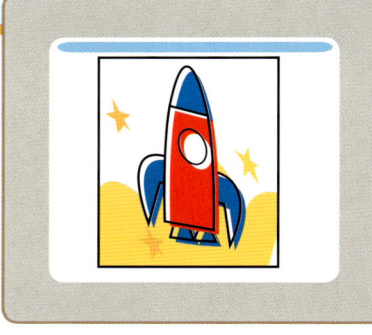

You could ask someone else to take a look at your work and tell you what they think.

File formats

If you're going to use your picture in a web page, presentation or word-processed document, you'll need to save it as the right type of file. Check what you need for your final piece of work.

If you're making a web page, for example, you'll need to save your picture as a .GIF or .JPEG file.

If you're pasting it into a word-processed project, it can be a .BMP file.

Last-minute changes

Even if your picture looks brilliant, is it the best it can be? Maybe it could be improved. You should always review your work, and perhaps change it to make it better.

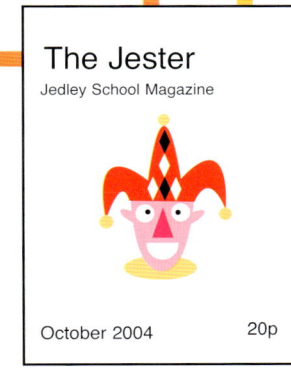

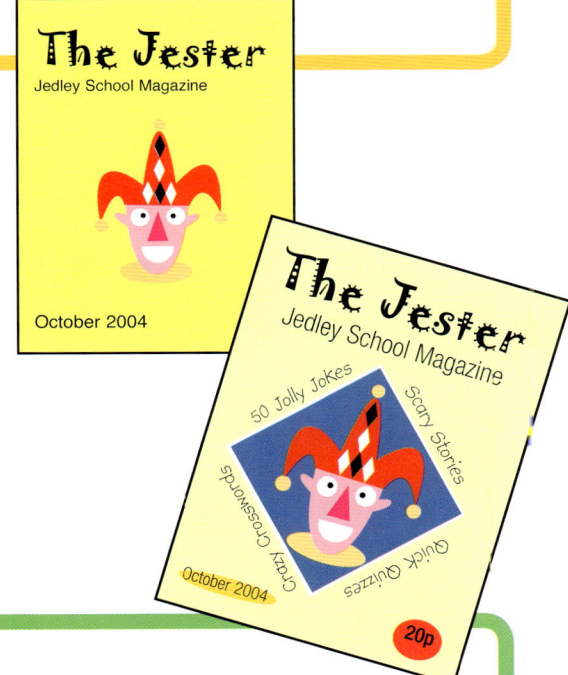

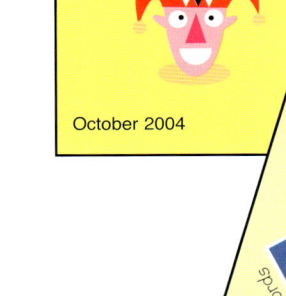

Finished!

When you've made any corrections or changes, save your work again before you print it out. Print one copy for a final check, before you print any extra copies you need.

SPREADSHEETS, GRAPHS AND CHARTS

What's it all about?

You've probably made models since you were small, using plastic bricks, cardboard or modelling clay. A model shows us what something looks like and how it works or behaves.

Computer models

You can also make **models** of a different kind on a computer. Computer models are useful in many areas of life. For example, architects, engineers and designers experiment with models, trying out different designs for buildings, bridges, vehicles and machinery.

Simulations

A **simulation** is a model of a process, such as a journey or an event. Computer simulations are used to plan trips by spacecraft, to teach pilots to fly planes, and to practise or experiment with other dangerous or expensive activities.

Spreadsheets

Governments and businesses use computers to model and plan spending and changes in society. Many of these models are made using spreadsheets – computer programs for working with numbers.

Work out how much money you can raise from a sponsored skate-boarding day.

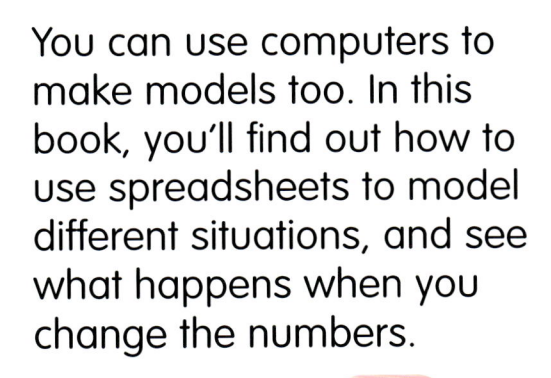

You can use computers to make models too. In this book, you'll find out how to use spreadsheets to model different situations, and see what happens when you change the numbers.

Find out how much paint you will need to buy to redecorate your room.

You'll also find out how to make a computer model do sums for you, how to put your results into a graph, and even how simulations and spreadsheets can help to forecast the future.

How does it work?

Spreadsheets are computer documents used for working with numbers. They let you make lots of calculations easily, and update all the answers instantly if you make any changes. They let you work out how things would be if you were to change any aspect of your plan.

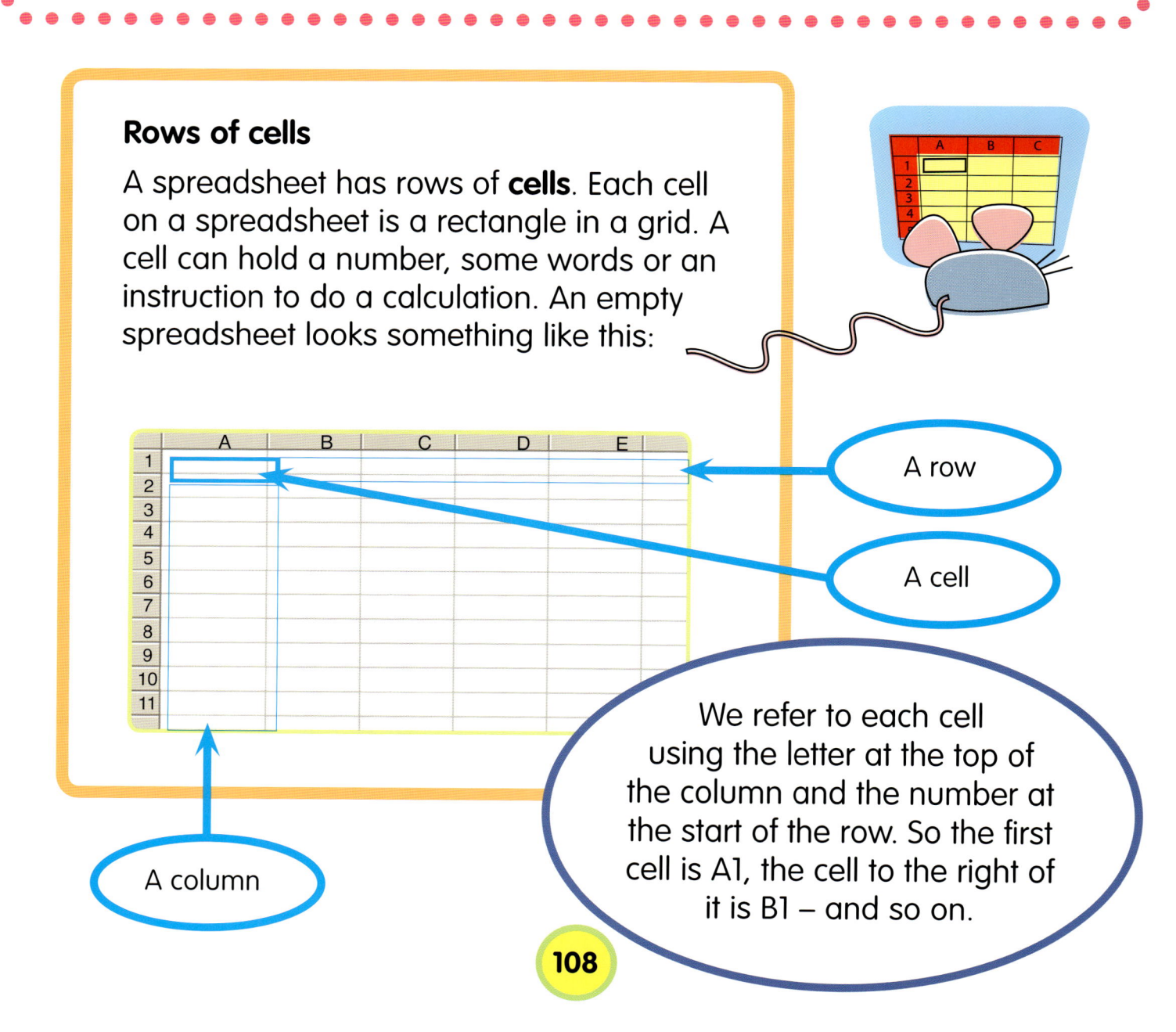

Rows of cells

A spreadsheet has rows of **cells**. Each cell on a spreadsheet is a rectangle in a grid. A cell can hold a number, some words or an instruction to do a calculation. An empty spreadsheet looks something like this:

A row

A cell

A column

We refer to each cell using the letter at the top of the column and the number at the start of the row. So the first cell is A1, the cell to the right of it is B1 – and so on.

When it's being used, a spreadsheet looks like this:

	A	B	C	D	E
1	**Pocket money modeller**				
2					
3	Alex gets		£ 2.50		
4	Fiona gets		£ 3.50		
5					
6	A remote controlled car costs				
7	£ 40.00				
8					
9	It will take Alex		16.0	weeks to save	
10	It will take Fiona		11.4	weeks to save	
11					

Plan your spending

This spreadsheet is a model of how someone might spend £10 of birthday money. It lists three items and their prices. The spreadsheet adds up the prices to give a total in a separate cell.

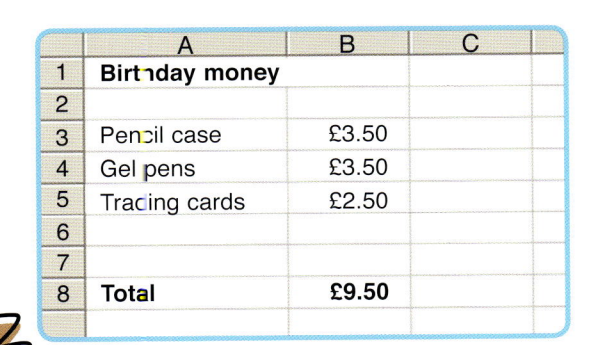

	A	B	C
1	**Birthday money**		
2			
3	Pencil case	£3.50	
4	Gel pens	£3.50	
5	Trading cards	£2.50	
6			
7			
8	**Total**	**£9.50**	

Making changes

Spreadsheets are useful because you can change the numbers and see different result. For example, if you were to change the second item from pens to a book, the computer would work out the sum again:

	A	B	C
1	**Birthday money**		
2			
3	Pencil case	£3.50	
4	Book	£3.99	
5	Trading cards	£2.50	
6			
7			
8	**Total**	**£9.99**	

Make your own spreadsheet

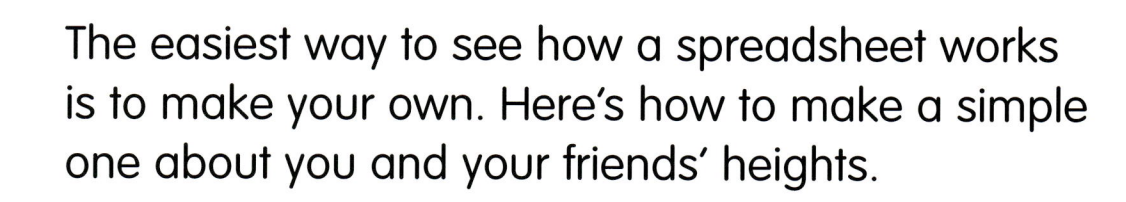

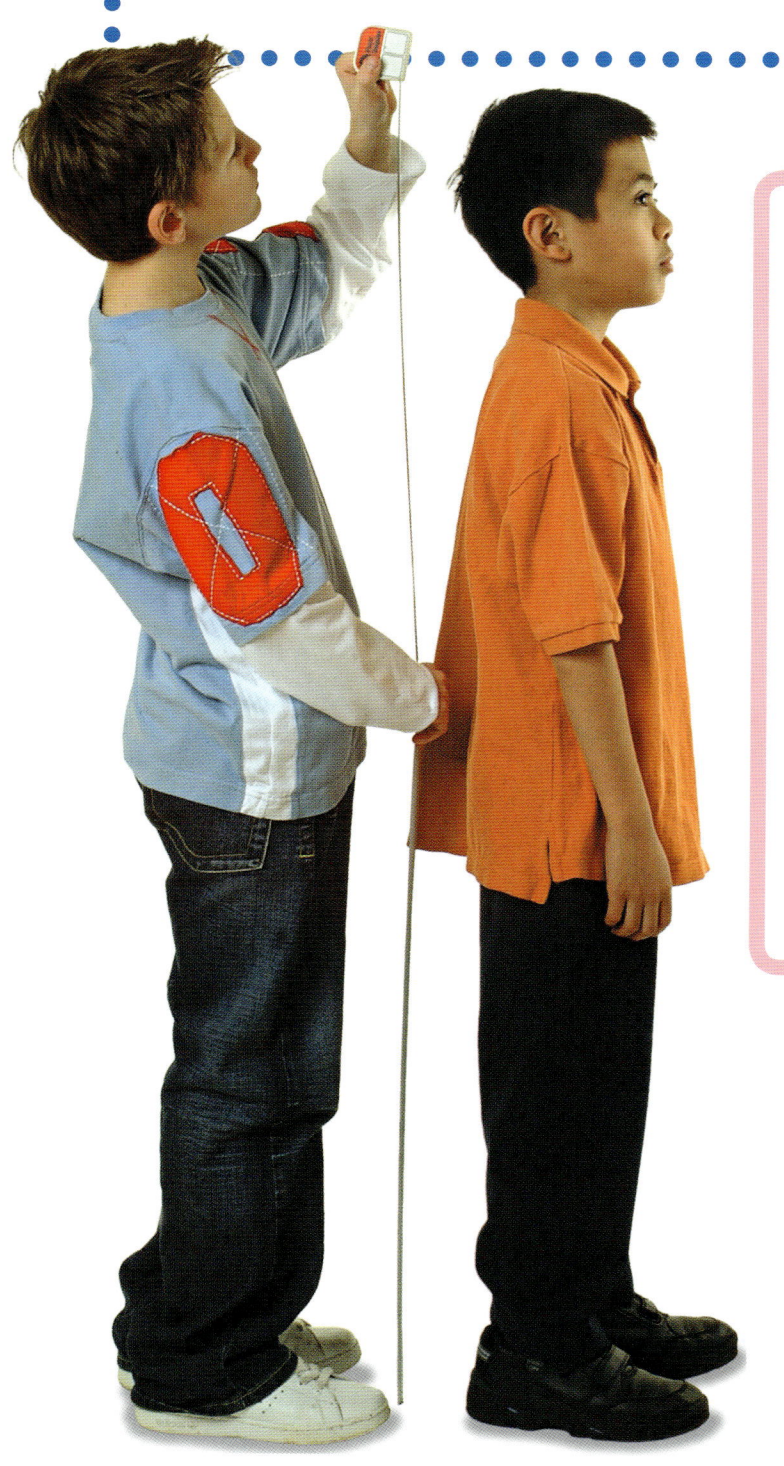

The easiest way to see how a spreadsheet works is to make your own. Here's how to make a simple one about you and your friends' heights.

Words and numbers

Using your spreadsheet software, start a new spreadsheet and click in the first cell. Type in the title:

How tall are we?

In the cells underneath, type a list of your friends' names. In the cell to the right of each name, put each person's height in centimetres (you can guess if you don't know).

	A	B	C
1	How tall are we?		
2			
3	Kate	124	
4	Luki	122	
5	Alex	135	
6	Sarah	131	
7	Max	136	
8	Helena	129	
9			

	A	B	C
1	How long are we?		
2			
3	Kate	124	
4	Luki	122	
5	Alex	135	
6	Sarah	131	
7	Max	136	
8	Helena	129	
9		777	
10			

Doing sums

So far, you've added text and numbers to the spreadsheet. Now it's time to make it do some work.

Click in cell B9, under the list of heights. Now type

=b3+b4+b5+b6+b7+b8

and press the Enter key.

This tells the spreadsheet to add up the numbers in cells B3–B8. It should change to show how long all of you would be, laid end to end.

If you want to check it, you can lie down with your friends and ask someone to measure you!

Using symbols

You tell a spreadsheet what to do using simple maths symbols called **operators**. In a spreadsheet, this kind of instruction is called a **formula**.

The equals sign =

tells the computer it has to work out the answer to a sum, and show this in the cell.

The formula we just used...

=b3+b4+b5+b6+b7+b8

...tells the spreadsheet to do a sum by adding the numbers in cells B3, B4, B5, B6, B7 and B8.

Another way to write this formula is

=sum(b3:b8)

This means 'add up all the numbers (find the 'sum' of the numbers) in cells B3 to B8'.

111

Working with data

The raw facts and figures that you put into a spreadsheet are called data. What you get out of a spreadsheet is information.

Yum yum!

Where does data come from?

The data you put into a spreadsheet usually comes from the world around you. It might come from a survey, such as asking your friends how many pets they have. Or you could collect data by doing an experiment – for example, by measuring people's heights, the temperature outside or recording the growth of your rabbit.

To get the right information out of a spreadsheet, the data you put in needs to be accurate (correct), and you need to make sure you use the right formulas.

Seed experiment

Imagine you're growing two trays of mustard and cress in two ways. You water one tray every day and the other every three days. Each day, you count how many seeds have sprouted. These measurements are your data.

You can tell just from this data that the seeds in tray 2 didn't grow as well. But by putting the data into a spreadsheet and making it do some sums, you can find out some more useful information:

Tray 1
2 4 9 14 17 17 18

Tray 2
0 2 4 6 7 7 6

	A	B	C	D	E	F	G	H
1		Day 1	Day 2	Day 3	Day 4	Day 5	Day 6	Day 7
2	Tray 1	2	4	9	14	17	17	18
3	Tray 2	0	2	4	6	7	7	6
4								
5	Difference	2	2	5	8	10	10	12

By subtracting tray 2's numbers from tray 1's numbers, the spreadsheet can show the difference between the trays.

DO IT!

To work out the difference between the trays the formula for cell B5 is:

On day 1:   **=B2-B3**

On day 2:   **=C2-C3**

and so on.

Remember to start each formula with an equals sign.

Other symbols are:

* for 'multiply'   **/** for 'divide'

Sorting it out

A big spreadsheet can have lots of data in it. It's often easier to spot patterns and find out facts if the data is listed in a particular order. Luckily, a spreadsheet can arrange your data in any order you like.

Paper problems

Suppose you'd listed the heights of a group of people on paper. You might write them down in the order in which you measured people. So if you wanted to find the tallest person, you'd have to check every number on the list. That's easy with a short list – but what if you'd listed everyone in your school?

How tall are we?

Luki	122
Kate	124
Helena	129
Sarah	131
Alex	135
Max	136

How tall are we?

Alex	135
Helena	129
Kate	124
Luki	122
Max	136
Sarah	131

If you wanted to put the list on the notice board in alphabetical order of name, or in order of height, you'd need to copy it all out again.

All in order

A spreadsheet can sort your data in any order you like at the click of a button. So you could put your friends in order of increasing or decreasing height, or in alphabetical order of name. And you can change the list around as many times as you like without having to do any more work!

	A	B	C
1	Where we come from		
2		Class 5B	
3	UK	20	
4	USA	2	
5	Africa	3	
6	Italy	2	
7	Sweden	1	
8			
9			

	A	B	C
1	Longest rivers		
2		Km	
3	Nile	6670	
4	Amazon	6404	
5	Chang Jiang	6378	
6	Huang He	5463	
7	Ob-Irtysh	5410	
8	Amur	4415	
9			

	A	B	C
1	Favourite drinks		
2		Votes	
3	Cola	10	
4	Lemonade	7	
5	Fruit juice	6	
6	Milkshake	4	
7	Water	3	
8	Tea	1	
9			

DO IT!

Look for an option to 'Sort' or 'Order' your data. Pick the column or row you want to use for sorting – such as names or heights. You can also choose whether to sort in ascending order (0–9 or a–z) or descending order (9–0 or z–a).

Graphs and charts

It's often even easier to see what's going on, and to check your data is correct, if you can see it in the form of a graph or chart. Spreadsheets can do this for you, too.

Bars, pies and lines

There are several types of graph or chart. You need to pick one that suits what you're doing.

Bar charts

A **bar chart** is a good way of showing numbers in different categories. This bar chart shows how many birds Luke saw in his garden between 8.00 and 8.30 every day for a week.

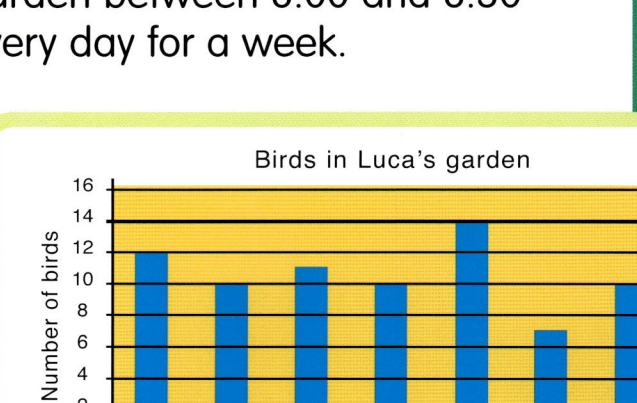

Birds in Luca's garden

Sometimes a chart can help you spot errors in your data. You might need to check your readings, or make sure that you copied the data into the spreadsheet accurately.

116

Pie charts

If you want to show proportions, a **pie chart** is best. This pie chart shows how children travel to school. It's easy to see at a glance how the class is divided.

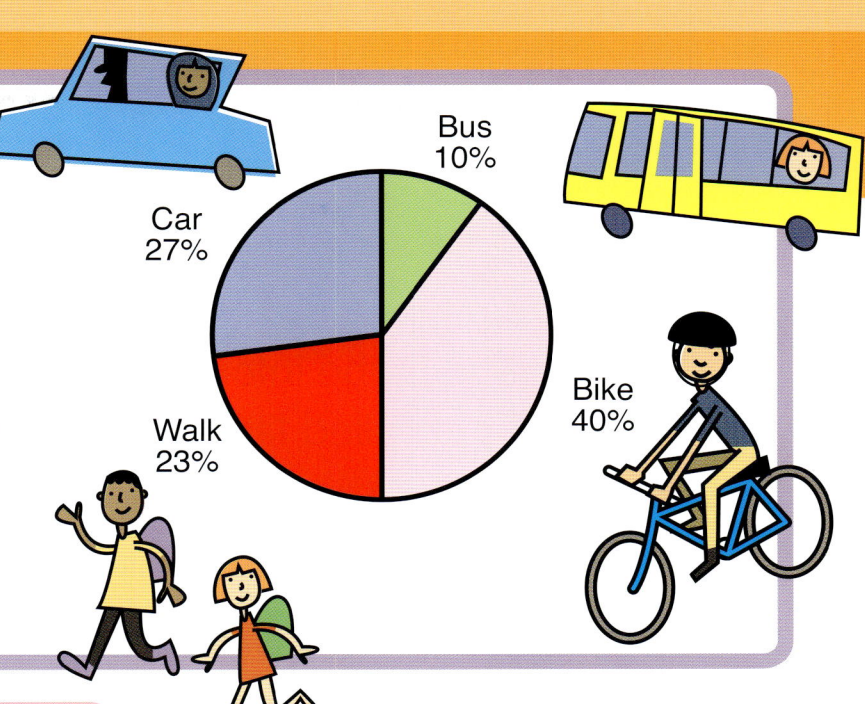

Car 27%
Bus 10%
Bike 40%
Walk 23%

Pictograms

You can also use a **pictogram**. This shows piles of the things you are counting, such as how many ice-creams you're allowed per week:

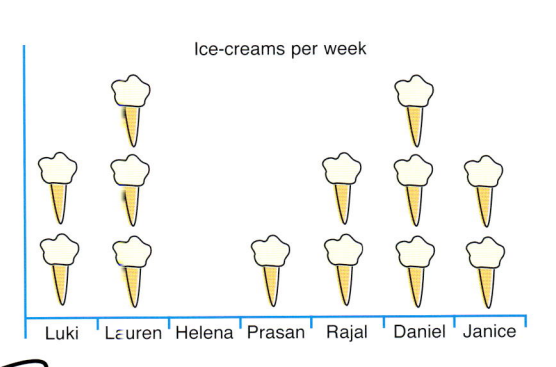

Ice-creams per week

Luki | Lauren | Helena | Prasan | Rajal | Daniel | Janice

Line graphs

A **line graph** is best if you have data made up of occasional readings. For instance, if you weighed a puppy once a week over three months, you could show the results as a line graph. The puppy grows all the time, but you don't measure it all the time. The line fills in the gaps.

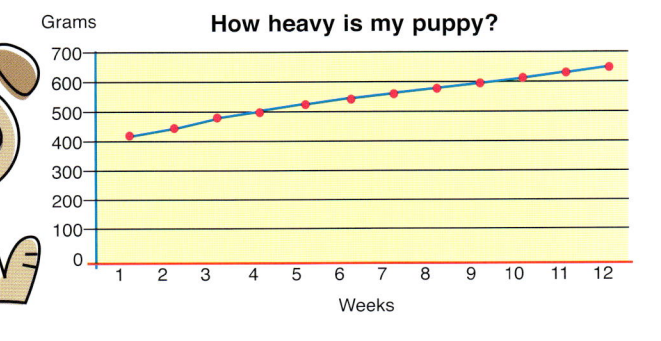

Grams — How heavy is my puppy?
Weeks

Filtered facts

It's often useful to be able to pick out only some of the information in your spreadsheet. This is called filtering your data.

In the sun

Here's an example of how you might **filter** useful data. This spreadsheet shows how many hours of sunshine you can expect each day in different holiday resorts during the summer.

	A	B	C	D	E	F
1	Pick a holiday					
2				Hours of sunshine in		
3	Resort code	Country	June	July	August	September
4						
5	AB01	Italy	9	10	11	9.5
6	AB02	France	8	9.5	9.5	7.5
7	AB03	Spain	9	10.5	11	10
8	EC01	Turkey	10	12	12	11
9	EC02	Spain	8	9	10	8.5
10	EC03	Turkey	11	12.5	12	11.5
11	RG04	Italy	10	11	11	10.5
12	RG06	France	7	8	9	8
13	EW03	Germany	6	6	7	6.4
14	EW06	Italy	9	10.5	11	10
15	NU12	Spain	8	9.5	10.5	10
16	NU14	France	7	8.5	9	8
17	ZX02	Italy	10	11.5	11	10
18	ZX03	Turkey	10.5	11.5	12.5	11

Where?

If you'd decided to go to Italy, you could ask the spreadsheet to show you only the information for Italy.

	A	B	C	D	E	F
1	Pick a holiday					
2				Hours of sunshine in		
3	Resort code	Country	June	July	August	September
4						
5	AB01	Italy	9	10	11	9.5
11	RG04	Italy	10	11	11	10.5
14	EW06	Italy	9	10.5	11	10
17	ZX02	Italy	10	11.5	11	10

When?

Or, if you were planning a holiday in August, you could ask your spreadsheet to show you only resorts that would have more than ten hours of sunshine a day in August.

	A	B	C	D	E	F
1	Pick a holiday					
2				Hours of sunshine in		
3	Resort code	Country	June	July	August	September
4						
5	AB01	Italy	9	10	11	9.5
7	AB03	Spain	9	10.5	11	10
8	EC01	Turkey	10	12	12	11
9	EC02	Spain	8	9	10	8.5
10	EC03	Turkey	11	12.5	12	11.5
11	RG04	Italy	10	11	11	10.5
14	EW06	Italy	9	10.5	11	10
15	NU12	Spain	8	9.5	10.5	10
17	ZX02	Italy	10	11.5	11	10
18	ZX03	Turkey	10.5	11.5	12.5	11

Making filters

To filter data, you pick the column or row you want to use, then tell the spreadsheet what to look for. You can ask for exact matches, or a range of data.

You need to use **operators** to tell the spreadsheet the range of numbers you want to look for. If you chose the 'August' column, for example, you could then use these operators to filter the data:

equals =

=10
will find all resorts that expect exactly ten hours of sunshine

more than >

>10
will find resorts with more than ten hours of sunshine

less than <

<10
will find resorts with less than ten hours of sunshine

DO IT!

Look for an option to 'Filter' your spreadsheet. You might be able to choose more than one thing to look for – for example:

Country = Italy AND August =>10

would look for resorts in Italy that had ten or more hours of sunshine a day in August.

Simulations

A simulation is a model of a real-life event or process. You might have played computer games that are simulations.

Types of simulations

There are lots of different types of simulation games – driving, flying a spaceship, keeping pets, building empires...

A simulation game might let you build and manage an imaginary zoo...

Or keep just one little virtual pet.

A simulation isn't as complicated as real life, but it can still be a very useful place to practise.

Imaginary worlds

Simulations aren't just for fun. They can be used to teach people real, important skills. For example, people learning to fly planes start by learning with simulators, so they can make mistakes safely.

Spreadsheets for modelling

The type of models in a simulation game are very complicated. Much simpler simulation models can be made with numbers in a spreadsheet.

Governments and organizations use spreadsheet models to work out complicated things, like how much money to spend on schools or how to evacuate people in an emergency. They break down problems into lots of sums, and see how the results change when different things happen.

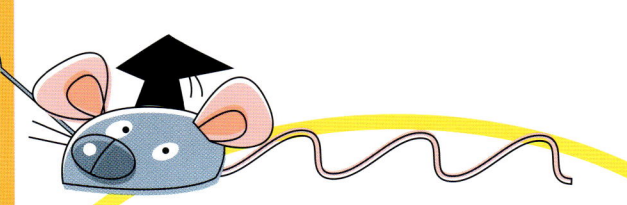

Working with money

A budget is the money available for a project. Your school has a budget – a fixed amount it can spend on books, teachers, new buildings and so on.

Budget model

If you plan a party, you might have a budget for that. You can use a spreadsheet to show you how you could spend the money in different ways. This spreadsheet shows how many guests you could have with a £40 budget and two possible menus.

	A	B	C	D	E
1	Party planner				
2					
3	Menu A (per person)			Menu B (per person)	
4	Pizza	£ 0.90		Curry	£ 0.65
5	Juice	£ 0.45		Rice	£ 0.20
6	Ice-cream	£ 0.70		Poppadum	£ 0.25
7	Crisps	£ 0.35		Juice	£ 0.45
8				Mango	£ 0.65
9		£ 2.40			£ 2.20
10					
11	Budget	£ 40.00			
12					
13	Number of people				
14					
15	Menu A		16.7		
16	Menu B		18.2		

All change!

One of the main reasons computer models are so useful is that you can make changes and see how things would work out in real life.

Planning and design

Designers and other professionals often use models to test their plans. For example, an engineer designing a bridge will use a computer model to see what would happen if heavy traffic crossed the bridge, or if a hurricane hit it.

Using simulations

If you play a simulation game, or if there is a simulation program you can use at school, you can make choices and see what happens as you do different things. For example, a skateboarding simulation game will show you what happens if you skateboard too fast – sooner or later, you'll fall off!

Planning

People use spreadsheet models to help them make decisions and plan. Imagine a toy company has decided to make a new range of plastic monsters. They know how many monsters they can sell at different prices, so they use a spreadsheet to find out how much money they'd make at each price:

They sell more monsters if they're cheaper – so the model tells them they'll make the most money by selling their monsters at £5.99.

£5.99

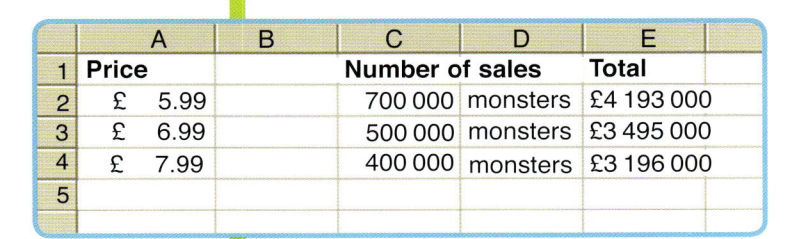

	A	B	C	D	E
1	Price		Number of sales		Total
2	£ 5.99		700 000	monsters	£4 193 000
3	£ 6.99		500 000	monsters	£3 495 000
4	£ 7.99		400 000	monsters	£3 196 000
5					

Change your party plans

You have already seen how to make a spreadsheet for a party budget. But what if you managed to make a cheaper curry for your party? You could change the cost of curry and the spreadsheet would do the sums again.

	A	B	C	D	E
1	Party planner				
2					
3	Menu A (per person)			Menu B (per person)	
4	Pizza	£ 0.90		Curry	£ 0.50
5	Juice	£ 0.45		Rice	£ 0.20
6	Ice-cream	£ 0.70		Poppadum	£ 0.25
7	Crisps	£ 0.35		Juice	£ 0.45
8				Mango	£ 0.65
9		£ 2.40			£ 2.05
10					
11	Budget	£ 40.00			
12					
13					
14	Number of people				
15	Menu A		16.7		
16	Menu B		19.5		

How many people?

Or you could work out how much it would cost to have different numbers of people, using each menu:

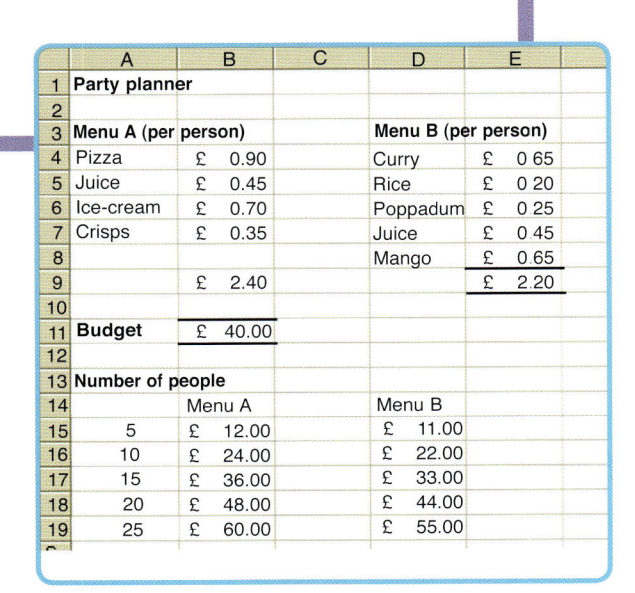

	A	B	C	D	E
1	Party planner				
2					
3	Menu A (per person)			Menu B (per person)	
4	Pizza	£ 0.90		Curry	£ 0.65
5	Juice	£ 0.45		Rice	£ 0.20
6	Ice-cream	£ 0.70		Poppadum	£ 0.25
7	Crisps	£ 0.35		Juice	£ 0.45
8				Mango	£ 0.65
9		£ 2.40			£ 2.20
10					
11	Budget	£ 40.00			
12					
13	Number of people				
14		Menu A		Menu B	
15	5	£ 12.00		£ 11.00	
16	10	£ 24.00		£ 22.00	
17	15	£ 36.00		£ 33.00	
18	20	£ 48.00		£ 44.00	
19	25	£ 60.00		£ 55.00	

Finding patterns

If there's a pattern or trend in a set of data, models can help us work out what's likely to happen next.

Weather modelling

Weather forecasts are an example of using models to predict what's going to happen. Meteorologists (people who study weather) keep records of the weather and look for patterns. These patterns are used to make computer models that can work out what the weather's likely to do next.

Number patterns

You can use a spreadsheet to see patterns in numbers, too. This spreadsheet shows the nine times table, up to 12 x 9.

You can see that in each of the numbers – 18, 27, 36 and so on – the digits add up to nine:

18 1 + 8 = 9
27 2 + 7 = 9
36 3 + 6 = 9

But does that always happen?

With a spreadsheet, it's easy to check. You can continue the spreadsheet up to any number you like. You'll find that from 21 x 9, the digits sometimes add up to 18 instead.

DO IT!

To make the nine times table spreadsheet, you'll need to put numbers counting upwards from 1 in column A. Then in cell B3 put the formula:

=a3*9

You can then use an option to 'Copy' or 'Replicate' this cell down the column. When you copy it, the spreadsheet changes the formula so that it's right in each row. So in cell B6, the formula will be:

=a6*9

If you wanted the spreadsheet to show the eight times table instead, you'd change the formula in B3 to:

=a3*8

and copy this into all the cells in the column.

Perfect!

If you use a spreadsheet in a project or to present the results of an experiment, make sure it's clear and easy for other people to understand.

Nice and clear

When you first make a spreadsheet, what you're doing is fresh in your mind, so you might not think you need to label the cells. But later, when you've done some other work, you might not remember what your spreadsheet shows.

A spreadsheet like this, that's just numbers with no titles or labels, won't mean much to you – and it certainly won't make sense to anyone else!

	A	B	C
1	03 June		3
2	10 June		2
3	17 June		0
4	24 June		1

	A	B	C	D
1	Basketball scores			
2				
3	Match date		Points we scored	
4	03 June		3	
5	10 June		2	
6	17 June		0	
7	24 June		1	

So remember to add clear, accurate labels like these as you make each spreadsheet.

Is it right?

As long as you put the right data into a spreadsheet, and give it the right instructions, it will give you the right answers. But if you make a mistake, it will go wrong. Always do a few rough calculations to make sure the answers in your spreadsheet make sense.

Here are some of the reasons a spreadsheet can go wrong:

- You've made a mistake putting your data into the spreadsheet, like putting numbers in the wrong order or missing something out. (Remember, making a graph can help you spot errors like this.)

- You've used the wrong formulas.

- You've mixed up different units (putting some lengths in metres and some in centimetres, for instance).

Always check your work carefully when you put your data in, and when you look at the answers.

INVITES, POSTERS AND PRESENTATIONS

What's it all about?

We all communicate in lots of different ways. We chat on the phone, read, watch TV and videos, send emails and texts, and look at web pages. This book is all about communicating with written words.

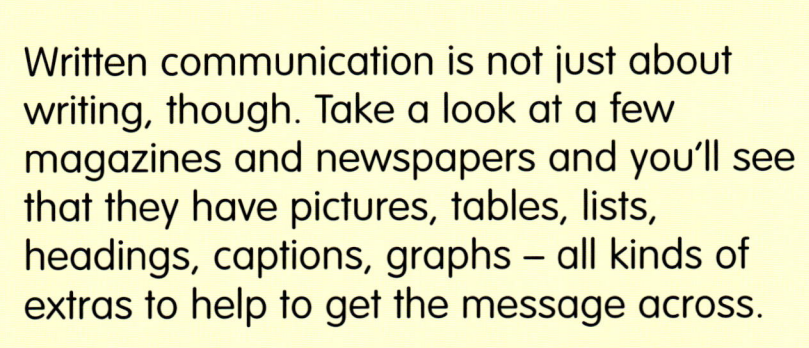

Written communication is not just about writing, though. Take a look at a few magazines and newspapers and you'll see that they have pictures, tables, lists, headings, captions, graphs – all kinds of extras to help to get the message across.

In this book, you'll learn to do the same – make your words lively and exciting, and arrange them so that they're easy to understand.

On paper or on screen?

You can write with a pencil or pen on a piece of paper – or you can write using a computer.

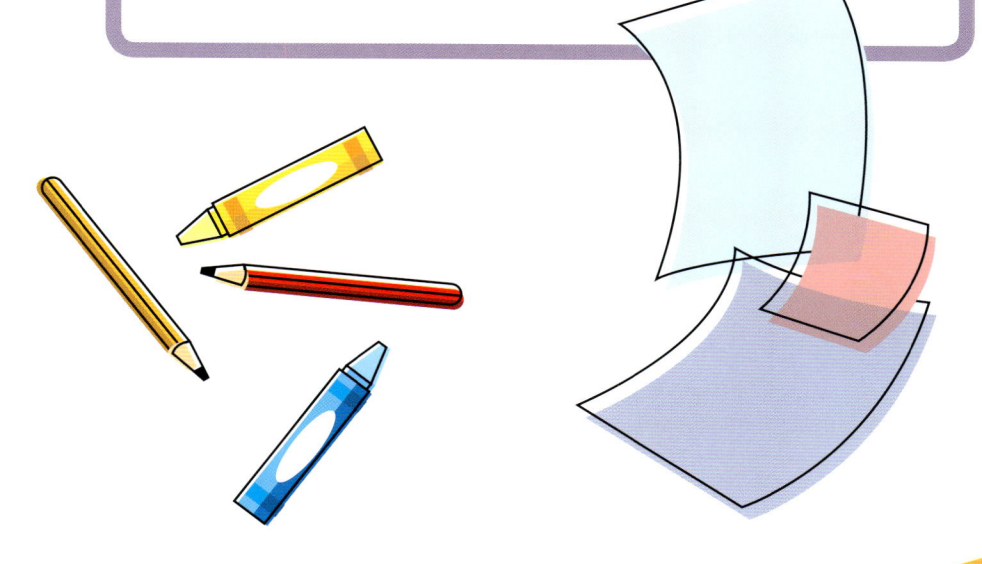

We're going to concentrate on writing on the computer using a word processor. But don't forget alternatives to the computer – sometimes paper and pens are still the best way!

How does it work?

Think before you speak – and before you write! You can save yourself a lot of work if you know what you're trying to do before you start.

Who, what, why?

Here are some things to ask yourself before you begin:

- What do I want to say?
- Who do I want to say it to?
- Why am I saying it at all?

What you want to say will be the **content** of your work. The people you want to say it to are your **audience**. Why you are saying it is your **purpose**.

We need to tell people how to find our new house in time for the party!

All our family and friends need to know... Otherwise they'll get lost!

It needs to be simple enough for everyone to read...

What will the content be?

Work out what you want to say before you start, so you can make sure you've included everything you need. Only say things that are relevant and don't wander off on a different topic.

Who's the audience?

You need to match your words and the way they're arranged (the **layout**) to what your audience expects and can read. If you say it in the wrong way, people might not understand or take notice. For example, you wouldn't use the same words in a report for your teacher as in an email to your seven-year-old cousin.

Why am I saying it?

The purpose of your writing will help you to decide what type of document to make and what extras to put in it. You might want to use a picture, a table or a chart to help get your message across. If you want to give people directions, for example, you could add a map.

Let's add a map to make it really clear!

We can post a printout to Auntie Abigail, and email it to everyone else!

How to find our house

Our house is at the end of Long Lane, off the High Street. It does not have a housenumber.

High Street

Long Lane

Getting started

Should you be using the computer at all? For a birthday card, it might be easier just to draw it on a piece of paper. If it's important that the writing is really neat, or if it's a long document you might want to change later, a computer is best.

Here are some things to think about:

- If you create your work on the computer, you can change it easily.
- If you create your work on paper, you can add extra bits, like stickers and glitter, cut holes, add flaps ...
- It's easy to create a really impressive-looking document on the computer – and the words and letters will be perfectly neat.
- If you create a document on the computer, you can re-use all or part of it later in another document.

Remember that you can start your work on the computer and add extras, like drawings, after you've printed it out.

134

Make a plan

It's a good idea to plan the main points you want to make before you start writing, especially if you're doing a complicated piece of work. Then collect your ideas, notes and any source materials you need, and you're ready to go.

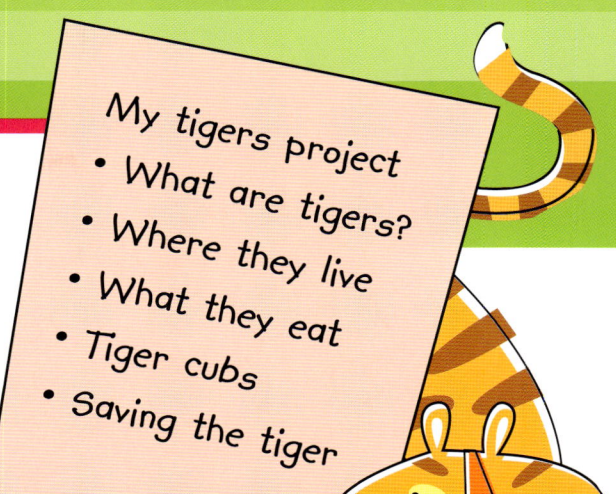

My tigers project
- *What are tigers?*
- *Where they live*
- *What they eat*
- *Tiger cubs*
- *Saving the tiger*

Starting to write

Once you've worked out what you want to say, you need to type it into the computer.

Remember to use:

- The space bar (once only) to add a space between words.

- The Shift key to get a capital letter.

- The Backspace key to get rid of a letter if you've typed the wrong one.

- The Enter or Return key to start a new line – but only when you get to the end of a paragraph, or a line in a list. The rest of the time, just keep typing: the computer will automatically start a new line for you when you need one.

Space bar

Shift key

Backspace key

Return key

Don't forget ... save your work often as you type it in, then you won't have to do it all again if anything goes badly wrong.

Making sense

All documents need to communicate a message, whether it's 'come to my party' or the details of your investigation of minibeasts. This means your document must make sense!

The right words for the right people

You should always write as clearly as you can, but sometimes you need to be extra careful to make things simple. Imagine there's been a flood in the school toilets, and you've been asked to make some posters warning people that the floor is wet.

If you were writing only for adults, you might put:

Beware! Danger of flooding

For little children, you would use simpler words that they would understand:

Look out! Wet floor!

A picture would make it even better, especially for smaller children:

Look out! Wet floor!

136

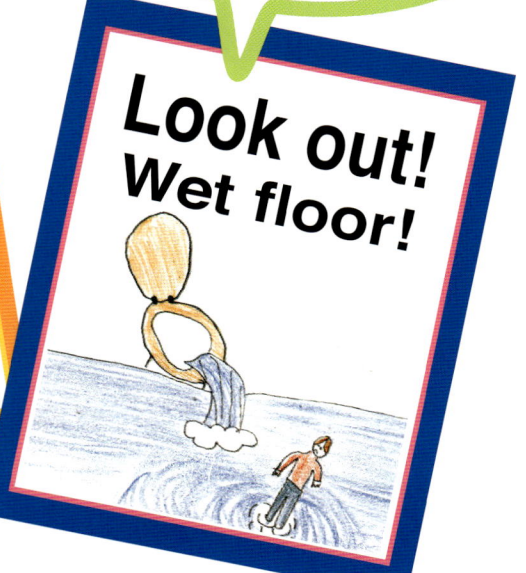

Putting things in order

Begin by working out the order you want to put your main points in. You should start with an introduction, then have a paragraph or section for each point, and finish by summing up what you've said.

Sometimes, the order is particularly important. If you're writing a set of instructions, you have to put the steps in the right order or else they won't work.

If your instructions for walking a dog didn't mention using the lead until the end, the dog could escape!

List of some things to do on our holiday

1 Go horse riding
2 Go swimming
3 Visit Castle
4 Cake shop

What matters most?

You may need to put items in order of importance, especially if you think some people might not read right to the end.

In a long piece of writing, you need to work out a good structure, so that people can find important ideas easily, and don't lose the thread of what they're reading.

If you're making a list, put the most important things first.

Organizing information

To make your documents easier to read, it helps to break down what you're saying into short chunks. It doesn't all have to be arranged in paragraphs either. Some information is easier to understand as a list or a table.

Headings and sections

To help people see where a long essay is going, you might divide it into sections with headings.

Each article in a newspaper or magazine has a heading so you can see what it's about. You'll need to do this if you're making a newsletter.

Don't forget a title for the whole document too, so that people know what they're about to read.

The solar system

The Sun

The Sun is just one of the trillions of stars in the Universe. It is in the middle of the solar system, and the planets revolve around it.

Mars

Mars is the fourth planet away from the Sun. It is smaller than the Earth and its gravity is not as strong. Mars looks red because of all the iron in its rocks.

The Jedley News

Bear bites man at Jedley zoo

New statue in park

Family day out

Big teeth

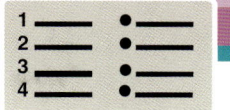

Lists

Sometimes a list is the best way to present information. To show a sequence of things, or the order of importance of several items, use a numbered list. If the order doesn't matter, you can use a list with bullets.

DO IT!

Look for a button for making a list with numbers or bullets. Select your text (see page 14), then click on the button. Or you can click the button first, then start typing your list.

Planning an experiment

1. Work out your aim
2. Choose your equipment
3. Carry out the experiment
4. Work out your conclusion

Equipment

You will need:

- A tub of earth
- Three worms
- Some leaves
- Water

Make a table

A table lines up text in columns and rows. It lets you show lots of facts or figures in a small space.

DO IT!

Look for an option to 'Insert Table', 'Add Table' or 'Draw Table'. Alternatively, you can use the Tab key to line up your text or numbers in columns.

How people in class 4X travel to school:

	Bike	Car	Walk	Bus	Total
Girls	7	5	4	1	17
Boys	6	7	3	0	16
Total	13	12	7	1	33

Looking good

The way your text looks should suit the audience and purpose of the document. Really wacky lettering and lots of colours might be great for a party invitation or poster, but they're not so good in a report on a science project.

Think about:

- The style, colour and size of the letters you're using.
- Using pictures to illustrate your text.
- Putting in headings and other special kinds of text.
- The way the pictures and words are arranged on the page.

Selecting text

You'll need to select text in order to change the way it looks.

1. Put the **cursor** at the start of the text you want to select.

2. Press and hold down the mouse button and move the mouse so that the text is highlighted.

3. Lift your finger off the mouse button when all the text you want is highlighted.

You can usually select all the text in your document at once, too. Look for a menu option called 'Select All'.

One part of this text has been selected. It is the type that is white on black instead of black on white.

Trial and error

Don't be afraid to experiment! It's easy to change things on a computer. Save different versions of your work with different names, so you can compare your designs and pick the best one.

Fun with fonts

The **font** is the style and shape of the letters. There might be lots of different fonts on your computer – take a look.

Pick the right font

Some fonts are easier to read than others. Fancy or dramatic fonts are good for making small bits of text stand out. Simple, clean-looking fonts are better for long blocks of text, as they're easier to read.

Picture fonts

Your computer might have some fonts that show little pictures. These are symbol fonts. You can use them to add symbols or pictures to your work. Because they are text, you can make them bigger or smaller by changing the text size.

Good for posters

Good for long essays

Text effects, styles and sizes

You can use special effects and different font styles and sizes to help get your message across.

Text effects

Try out different effects and styles to make your text more exciting.

These words are bold

These words are italic

These are underlined

These are outlined

These are shadowed

Changing colour

You can change the colour of your text. Just select the text, and click on a colour from the colour menu.

Remember that your colours will only show up on a printout if you're using a colour printer. Otherwise, they'll come out grey.

DO IT!

Select the text you want to change. Look for a menu option such as 'Font', 'Text style' or 'Text effects', and buttons that show the style of text you want, like this:

B *I* U O S

class of 2009

MARIA
Class joker
"You've got something on your face – oh, it's your nose."

RAJ
Future NASA scientist
"3... 2... 1... Liftoff!"

MAX
Head in the clouds
"Is it 2009 already?"

ANNA
Teacher's fave
"I can't believe we're leaving!"

Text size

Text size is usually shown in **point size**. This is a special measurement that comes from old-style printing. There are 72 points in an inch (2.5cm). The text in this book is 14 point – a good size for the main text of a long piece of writing.

SCHOOL REPORT
This is my report on 10-point text. 10-point text is quite small, so it's perfect if you want to fit in lots of words. To make it easy to read, it helps to break your text up into short paragraphs.

Please come to my 20-point text party

DO IT!

Select the text you want to change. Look for a box where you can type in the text size you want, or a menu offering different sizes you can choose.

BEWARE 36 POINT TEXT

Say what you mean

Try using different colours, sizes and styles to add to or emphasize the meaning of your words.

computer

splash

fancy

prickle

thin

spooky

growth

sport

Pictures

Most documents look better with pictures, or diagrams to help explain things. Sometimes, the picture can be the most important part of all.

Where do I get pictures?

You can get pictures onto the computer in lots of ways.

- If you have a digital camera, you can take a digital photo and load it into the computer.
- If you have a scanner, you can scan in pictures you've drawn on paper.
- You can use an art program on the computer to paint or draw a picture.
- You can use clip art – ready-made pictures that you can get on CD-ROM or from the World Wide Web.

The solar system

The Sun

The Sun is just one of the trillions of stars in the Universe. It is in the middle of the solar system, and the planets revolve around it.

Mars

Mars is the fourth planet away from the Sun. It is smaller than the Earth and its gravity is not as strong. Mars looks red because

Placing a picture

Think carefully about where on the page you want your picture to be, and how big it should be. Keep pictures near the text they go with.

Sometimes, the picture is the biggest thing on the page.

LOST!

Have you seen Alice?

DO IT!

Look for an option like 'Insert picture', 'Insert clip art' or 'Add picture'. There might be some drawing tools in your text program that let you draw a simple picture straight onto the page.

If you save a picture you've made on the computer, make sure it's a type of file your word processor can read. You might need to ask for help with this.

Do it by hand

Don't forget you can draw extra things on the page after you've printed your work out. So if you don't have a scanner or art program, you can just leave a space on the page and fill it in later.

Picture sizes

If you need to make a picture bigger or smaller when it's in your document, look for little blocks, called 'handles', at the corners of the picture, and click on and drag these to change the size.

You can also move a picture around by clicking on the middle of it and dragging it.

If you drag a handle on a side, rather than a corner, your picture might become squashed or stretched.

Arranging text

The way text is arranged, lined up and spaced affects how good it looks and how easy it is to read.

Text alignment

Alignment means the way the text lines up between the edges of the page. Most of the text in this book is left-aligned.

Titles are often **centred**, which means they are lined up in the middle of the page.

This line is centred

Picture captions are sometimes right-aligned. They line up at the ends of the lines, on the right-hand side of the page.

This line is right-aligned

Keep it clear

Centred text and right-aligned text are good for special effects but they're quite hard to read, so don't over-use them.

DO IT!

Look for buttons with pictures of text alignments, like these:

Or look for options like 'Align Text', 'Right Align' or 'Center Text'.

Solar System News

Moon landing planned
Astronauts are planning to set foot on the Moon again. It will be the first trip to the Moon for over 30 years.

Solar flares
The Moon
Scientists have reported that solar flares have been extra-large and extra-strong in recent months. They can affect computers and make them stop working.

Different styles for different sections

If you look at a magazine or book, you'll see that lots of different styles of text are used for different types of text. You can use different styles of text in your own work too. Try to match the way the text looks with how important that part is.

Minibeasts

Minibeasts get their name because they're smaller than most other animals. They include insects, spiders, worms, slugs and snails.

Minibeasts without legs
Many minibeasts have no legs at all. They simply slide, slither or burrow their way around.

A giant African land snail

Snails
A snail moves along the ground by rippling the underside of its body. It also releases a slippery slime to help it move.

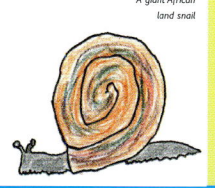

Worms
Worms' bodies are made up of segments.

Headings and subheadings

Your main heading should be bigger than the subheadings that split the text up. Make headings look striking by changing the **font**, text size and colour. Don't forget you can use underlining, bold or other styles if you like.

Main text and other text

Pick a font, size and style for your main text, then choose other styles for other types of text. For example, you could use a big, bold style for the introduction to help your readers get started.

Staying the same

When you use different styles, make sure you use them consistently. This means always using the same font and style for text of the same sort – captions, for example.

WATCH OUT!
Don't use too many different fonts and colours, as your work will start to look messy and it will distract people from what your document says.

Page layout

The way your document is arranged on the page is called the layout. By putting text in columns or adding space, you can make a document look better.

Margins and columns

Most documents have areas of white space around the edges of the page, called margins. Big margins give the page a more spacious look and make it easier for people to read. Putting text in two or more columns is effective if you're making a newsletter.

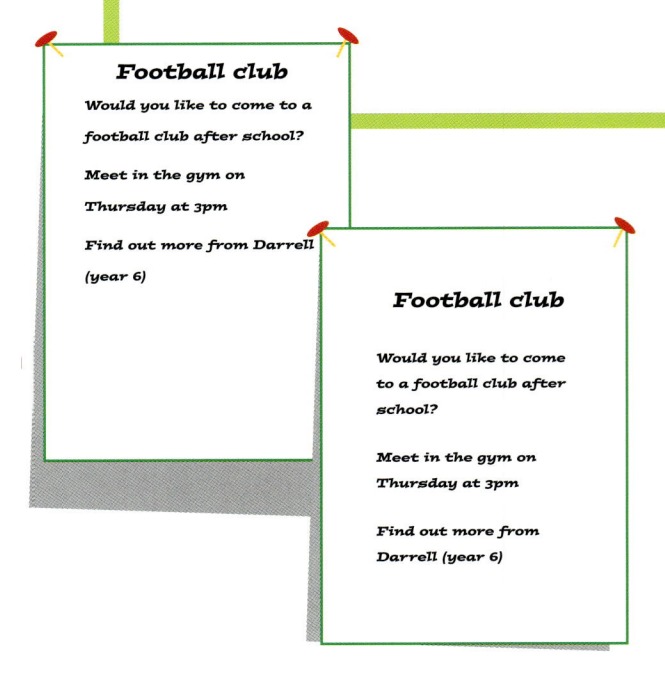

DO IT!

Look for a button or menu option called 'Columns' or 'Number of columns'.

Pictures and text

Think about where to put the pictures. They'll look better if they're spread out evenly through the text. If they're rectangular, line them up carefully so that they don't look too untidy.

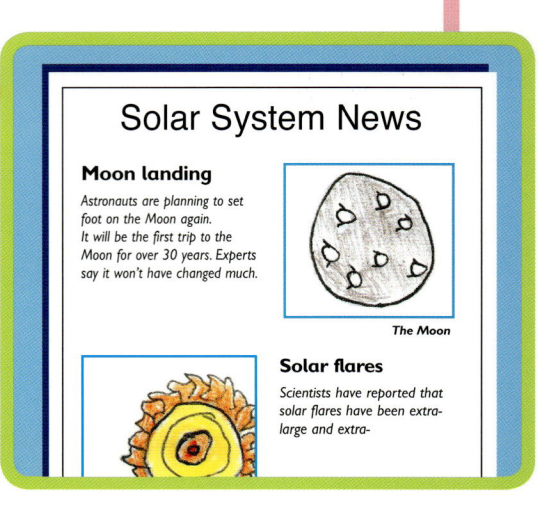

Football club

Would you like to come to a football club after school?

Meet in the gym on Thursday at 3pm

Find out more from Darrell (year 6)

Football club

Would you like to come to a football club after school?

Meet in the gym on Thursday at 3pm

Find out more from Darrell (year 6)

Solar System News

Moon landing

Astronauts are planning to set foot on the Moon again. It will be the first trip to the Moon for over 30 years. Experts say it won't have changed much.

The Moon

Solar flares

Scientists have reported that solar flares have been extra-large and extra-

Blank space

Empty space on the page is very helpful for your readers. It's hard to read words that are very cramped and crowded together. Leave space between paragraphs and around pictures, and make sure the margins are large enough.

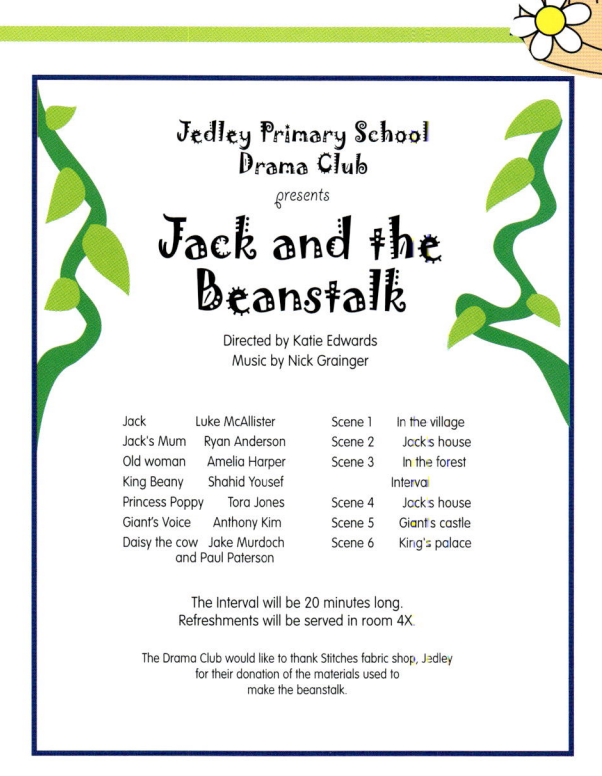

Jedley Primary School Drama Club presents
Jack and the Beanstalk

Directed by	Katie Edwards
Music by	Nick Grainger
Jack	Luke McAllister
Jack's Mum	Ryan Anderson
Old woman	Amelia Harper
King Beany	Shahid Yousef
Princess Poppy	Tora Jones
Giant's voice	Anthony Kim
Daisy the cow	Jake Murdoch and Paul Paterson

Scene 1	In the village
Scene 2	Jack's house
Scene 3	In the forest
Interval	
Scene 4	Jack's house
Scene 5	Giant's castle
Scene 6	King's palace

The Interval will be 20 minutes long.
Refreshments will be served in room 4X.
The Drama Club would like to thank Stitches fabric shop, Jedley for their donation of the materials used to make the beanstalk.

Jedley Primary School Drama Club presents
Jack and the Beanstalk

Directed by Katie Edwards
Music by Nick Grainger

Jack	Luke McAllister	Scene 1	In the village
Jack's Mum	Ryan Anderson	Scene 2	Jack's house
Old woman	Amelia Harper	Scene 3	In the forest
King Beany	Shahid Yousef		Interval
Princess Poppy	Tora Jones	Scene 4	Jack's house
Giant's Voice	Anthony Kim	Scene 5	Giant's castle
Daisy the cow	Jake Murdoch and Paul Paterson	Scene 6	King's palace

The Interval will be 20 minutes long.
Refreshments will be served in room 4X.

The Drama Club would like to thank Stitches fabric shop, Jedley for their donation of the materials used to make the beanstalk.

DO IT!

To set the space around the page, look for an option like 'Set margins', 'Page margins', 'Page setup' or 'Page layout'.

To add space between paragraphs or pictures, use the Enter or Return key to add a blank line.

Perfect!

So you've entered all the words and made them look good, but your work's not quite done yet. You need to review it and see if you can improve it.

Ask for help

It's not always easy to judge how good your own work is, so it's a good idea to get a friend, parent or other checker to look at it, too. You – and your checker – should ask:

- Does the document get across the message I wanted it to effectively?
- Are the words suited to the **audience** and purpose?
- Does it look right?
- How could I make my work even better?

Making changes

Maybe your work would be better if parts of it were moved around. To move a chunk of text, you'll need to:

1. Select the text you want to move.

2. Choose a 'Cut' button or menu option to cut the text.

3. Put the cursor to where you want to move the text.

4. Use a 'Paste' button or menu option to put the text back in.

Find and replace

If you want to change a word all the way through a document, you can use **find and replace**. For example, if you'd written a report on Julius Caesar, but typed his name in wrong, you could find all the times you had used 'Juluis' and change them to 'Julius'.

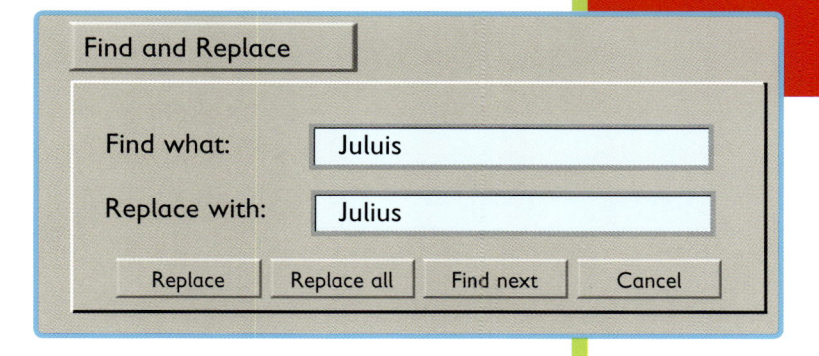

DO IT!

Look for a menu option such as 'Find and replace' or 'Search and replace'. Then just type in the words you want to find, and what you want to change them to.

Spellchecking

Your word processor may have a spellchecker. It checks the words you've used and compares them with its own dictionary. Look out – a spellchecker sometimes misses words that are spelled wrongly, or tells you a word is wrong even if it isn't, because it doesn't recognize it. If you use a spellchecker, check your work yourself too.

All finished

When you've improved and checked your work, you can print out your final copies. Save your work again before you print it, just in case anything goes wrong. Print just one copy first so that you can check it a final time, before you print any extra copies.

151

GLOSSARY

Address book
List of email addresses kept on your computer.

Attachment
Extra file sent with an email message.

Audience
The people who you hope will look at your work.

Bar chart
Chart in which the height of the columns (bars) shows the frequency or number of the thing being counted.

Bookmark
Saved reference to a web page you want to use again.

Cell
A single rectangle in the grid of a spreadsheet.

Classification system
Way of organizing information so that it's easy to find things.

Collage
Picture made up of pieces of other pictures and patterns, fabrics and even small objects.

Control sequence
Set of instructions that causes something to happen in response to an event.

Control technology
Electronic device or equipment that follows a set of instructions.

Digital camera
Camera that stores pictures in a computer chip rather than on a film.

Directory page
Web page that lists different topics to help you find a particular subject.

Electrical components
Wires, switches, bulbs, buzzers and other pieces of equipment that are used to make electrical circuits.

Favourite
Saved reference to a web page you want to use again.

Field
Space on a database record for a single item of information about something.

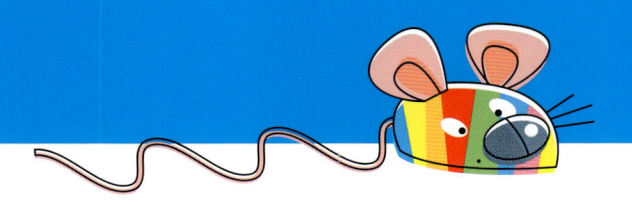

Filter
To extract a particular type or category of information from a spreadsheet or database.

Font
Style of letters; all the letters in a font have a similar appearance.

Formula
Instruction used to make a spreadsheet do a sum.

Handle
Block on the side or corner of a selected part of a picture; you can move the handles to change the size and shape of that part.

Hotspot
Part of a page you can click on to follow a link.

Hyperlink
Word or picture linked to another page.

Hypertext
System of interlinked pages of words and pictures.

Inbox
Place where email messages are stored when they arrive on your computer.

Input
Information coming in to a computer system.

Interactive
Able to respond to users actions or choices by, for example, playing a sound or displaying another page.

Internet
Network of computers connected together around the world so that they can share information.

Keyword
Word used to search the World Wide Web or another database.

Line graph
Graph made by adding lines between plotted points.

Logo
Programming language used to control a floor or screen turtle.

Loop
Set of instructions that can be repeated again and again.

Mailbox
Place where email messages are stored when they arrive on your computer.

Mass communication
A message intended for lots of people at once.

Model
A copy of a real object or scene, used to try out how it would look or work.

Mondrian
Piet Mondrian (1872-1944), a painter who made pictures from blocks of colour and lines.

Monitoring
Taking regular readings from a sensor to keep track of the state of something, such as the temperature or level of noise.

Object
Item in a drawing, like a shape or line, that can be moved on its own.

Online
Connected to the Internet, or on the World Wide Web.

Operator
Special symbol or word used in a spreadsheet formula or filter.

Output
Information or event that is produced by a computer at the end of a series of instructions.

Pictogram
A type of graph or chart that uses little pictures of the objects that are being counted.

Pie chart
Chart made by dividing up a circle to show proportions.

Pixel
Tiny dot on the computer screen.

Plan
Drawing that accurately represents something in the real world.

Pointillist
Type of painting made up of lots of tiny coloured dots.

Procedure
Set of instructions that together make something happen. A procedure is a chunk of a program.

Program (noun)
Set of instructions that make a computer do something.

Programming
Writing instructions to make a computer do something.

Purpose
The aim of your picture.

Query
Question that you ask of a database in order to find information.

Record
All the information about one particular item in a database.

Repeat (noun)
Set of instructions that can be repeated again and again.

Report
Printout or screen display of information found in a database.

Review
Look through and check.

Scale
Relationship between the size of an object in a drawing and in real life.

Scanner
Device for copying pictures from paper into the computer.

Search engine
Web page used to search the World Wide Web.

Sensor
Device for measuring the level of something, such as the temperature or the level of noise, pressure or movement.

Sequence
Series of items, such as musical sounds or notes.

Simulation
Model of a process or situation used to try things out on a computer.

Sort
To arrange information into a particular order.

Sound sample
Short recording of sound, such as speech, music or sound effects.

Trigger
Make something happen at a particular time.

Web browser
Computer program for looking at and moving between web pages.

INDEX

accuracy 52
address book 68–69
addresses
　email 64, 65
　home 63
alignment 146
architects 106
arranging text 146–147
art programs 144
attachments 70–71, 72
audience 75, 84, 132, 133

back button 48
background colors 87
Backspace key 135
bar charts 116
blank space 149
bold text 142
bookmarks 49
books 60
brackets 19
brain 34
browser 48
budgets 121
bullet points 139
buttons 67, 70, 74, 76, 78, 79

calculations 39, 106–109
rough calculations 127
captions 146, 147
CD-ROMs 36, 55, 72, 74, 77, 78

cells 106, 108
centred text 146
changes
　monitoring 27
　to paintings 88–89
　to pictures 90–91, 92
changing data 105, 107, 122, 123
charts 45, 116–117
checking 78–79, 150–151
checking facts 52–53
checking for mistakes 30–31
checking sensors 28, 29
checking work 79, 127
classification systems 37
clip art 78, 144
coded letters 60
colour 75, 142, 143
colour palette 86
columns 108, 148
communication 130–131
comparing facts 39
computer games 120, 122
computer graphics 83
computer programs 71, 72, 92
computers 34–35
　advantages 134
　keys 135
　content 132, 133
　control sequence 10–11

input and output 12–13
　testing 30
control technology 10, 26, 28
copy 125
copying 55, 88–89, 95, 99
cropping 91
cursor 140
cut and paste 150
cutting 88

data 112–115
　checking 127
　collecting 112–113
　filtering 118–119
　sorting 114–115
databases 35, 116
　building 40–41
　how they work 36
　searching for facts in 46–47
　starting 42–43
deleting 88
design 74–75
designers 106
designing, using models 101
developing "eye" 84
digital camera 90, 144
digital photos 90–91
directories 50
drawing shapes 18–19
drawing tools 93

drawings 85, 92–93, 134
   layering 96–97
   making changes to 94–95
   moving 92, 94
   on paper 82
dropdown menu 49
drums 60, 61

electrical components 25
emails 58, 61
   addresses 64, 65, 68–69
   attachments 70–71, 72
   printing out 66
   receiving 66–67
   replying to 67
   sending 64–65
   subject 65
encyclopaedias 34, 37
engineers 106, 122
Enter key 135
environment 11
   changes in 27
   monitoring 15
equipment 10

fact-finding 37, 39, 46–47
   on Web 50–51
favorites 49
fields 42–43
file formats 103
file types 79

filter 46, 118–119
find and replace 151
finding information 37, 39, 40–41, 46–47
   in database 46–47
   on Web 50–51
flags 60, 61
flip 89
flood fill 87
floor turtle 14, 16–17
flowchart 73
font 91, 141
formula 111, 113, 125

games 120, 122
getting started 134–135
graphs 45, 107, 116, 117
grid 99
grownups, help from 63, 71

handles 94, 95, 145
heating 10, 15, 29, 138, 147
height spreadsheet 110–111
highlighting 140
home button 48, 49
home page 48, 49
hotspots 72
house drawings 22
hyperlinks 72
hypertext 72

icons 74
inbox 66
index 37
input 12–13, 15, 26, 28
instructions 10, 11, 14–15
   mistakes 22, 23
   naming 19
   repeats 18–19
   for sequences 24–25
   testing 22–23, 30–31
   writing 16–19
Internet 48, 63
Internet Explorer 48, 49
italics 142

keywords 51

labels 126
law 55
layering 96–97
layout 148–149
learning skills 120
letters 60, 61
libraries 37
life support system 29
light switching 15
line graphs 117
lines 93
links 48, 49
lists 38–39, 139
Logo 17, 19
looking good 140–141
loop 18, 22
loyalty cards 36

157

machines 10
mailbox 66
making sense 136–137
margins 148, 149
mass communications 59, 60
meteorologists 100
mirror 89
mistakes 22, 23, 30–31, 86, 89
models 100–101, 106–107, 124
   making changes to 122, 123
Mondrian, Piet 87
monitoring 15, 27, 31
moving 88, 92, 94
moving text 150
multimedia 59, 62–63, 72–73
   adding pictures 78–79
   adding sound 76–77, 78, 79
   audience 75
   color 75
   creating 72–73
   design 74–75
   planning 73
multiple copies 89
music 76
mystery shape 21

neatness 134
Netscape 48, 49
newsletters 148
newspapers 60
number mistakes 23
number patterns 125
numbering 139
numbers 107, 108–111
   objects 85, 92, 93
   layering 96–97
   making changes to 94–95

online 72
operators 47, 119
order 115, 137
   changing 96, 97
organizing information 138–139
outline 142
output 12–13, 15, 28

page layout 148–149
painting tools 87
paintings 85, 86–87
   adding to 96
   making changes to 88–89
   moving 92
paper and pen 131
paper clip 70, 71
paper lists 38, 39
pasting 55, 88, 89, 95, 99

patterns 20–21, 95, 124–125
pendown 17, 23, 30
penup 17, 19, 21, 23, 30
photographs:
   changing 90
pictograms 117
picture fonts 141
pictures 55, 78–79, 144–145
   changing size 145
   layout 148
pie charts 117
pixels 86
planning 84, 123, 132–133, 135
plans 83, 98–99, 100
point size 143
Pointillist 87
PowerPoint 72
predicting future 107
presentations 83, 103
print preview 102
printing 66, 102, 103
printing out 39, 44, 54, 55
procedure 19, 22
programming 14
programs 14, 44
   testing 22–23
purpose 84, 132, 133

queries 46

radio 60
recording sound 77
records 42–43
rectangle 20
reflect 89
relevance 52, 53
reliability 52, 53
reordering information 44
repeating 83
repeats 18–19
replicate 125
reports 54
Return key 135
reviewing 102–103
reviewing work 150–151
rotate 89
rough calculations 127
rows 108

safety 63
save 89, 101, 103
saving
  attachments 71
  pages 79
  pictures 79
saving pages 55
saving work 135, 151
  pictures 145
scale 98
scanner/scanning 78, 82, 90
scanners 144
search engine 51

searching:
  database 46–47
  the Web 51
sections 138
security lights 28
selecting 88
selecting text 140
sensors 15, 26–27, 28–29
  checking 28, 29, 31
  connected to computer 27
sequences 24–25, 76
shadowed text 142
shapes 18–22
sharing information 54–55
Shift key 135
simulations 106, 107, 120–121
skills, simulations 120
smoke signals 60
snap 99
snowflakes 21
software 14
sorting 39, 44, 114–115
sound 76–77
sound effects 77
space 149
spacebar 135
spaces 17
speech bubbles 91
spellchecking 151

spelling mistakes 23
spreadsheets 107, 108–115
  calculations with 108–111
  cells 108
  changing data in 107, 109, 122, 123
  collecting data for 112–113
  columns 108
  filtering facts 118–119
  formula 111, 113, 125
  labelling 126
  number patterns 125
  reasons to go wrong 127
  rows 108
sprout experiment 113
sorting data 114–115
symbols 111
square 18–19
stealing 55
storing information 34–35
storyboard 25
street lighting 27
structure 137
subheadings 147
sums 107, 108–111
supermarket doors 12, 13, 15
surveys 40–41
switches 26

symbol fonts 141
symbols 47, 111, 119

tables 139
telephone 60, 61
television 60
temperature:
   control 15
   monitoring 27, 31
templates 101
text (words), adding 91, 93, 98
text messaging 61
text
   arranging 146–147
   effects 142
   fonts 141, 147
   moving 150
   selecting 140
   size 142, 143, 147
   style 142, 143, 147
thermostat controls 29
thought bubbles 91
time sequences 25
title 138
toolboxes 87, 93
traffic lights 24, 25
triangle 20
triggers 26–27, 29, 31
turtle 14, 16–17
typing 135
typing information 43

underlining 142
undo 89

weather forecasts 124
web address 48, 49
web browser 48
web pages 59, 72, 83, 103
   design 74–75
websites 72, 74
windmill 21
word-processed document 103
word-processing program 72
words, adding 91, 93, 98
World Wide Web 35, 48–51, 55, 63, 77, 78